The Flower Hunter
ELLIS ROWAN

Patricia Fullerton

National Library of Australia
Canberra 2002

Published by the National Library of Australia
Canberra ACT 2600
Australia

© National Library of Australia 2002

National Library of Australia Cataloguing-in-Publication entry

Fullerton, Patricia, 1945–.
The flower hunter: Ellis Rowan.

Bibliography
ISBN 0 642 10760 2.

1. Rowan, Ellis, 1848–1922—Exhibitions. 2. Wild flowers
in art—Exhibitions. 3. National Library of Australia
—Exhibitions.
I. Title.

759.994

Guest Curator: Patricia Fullerton assisted by
                Tim Fisher, Exhibitions Branch Curator
Designer: Kathy Jakupec
Editor: Francesca Rendle-Short
Printed by Brown Prior Anderson

Front cover: ***Barringtonia sp. with Larva*** c.1916–1917
         Papua New Guinea
         gouache and watercolour on paper;
         73.3 x 55.8 cm
         nla.pic–an23621170
         Pictures Collection R1761

A National Library of Australia
Travelling Exhibition

The tour of this exhibition is made possible by
Visions of Australia

FOREWORD

*The Flower Hunter: Ellis Rowan is dedicated to Mr Norman McCann (1948–2002),
Member of the National Library of Australia Council (1999–2002).*

The National Library of Australia is our country's largest library, and the repository of the nation's memory. Our collections of books, journals, newspapers and magazines, manuscripts, pictures, maps, music, films and videos, oral histories and online publications provide a comprehensive record of Australian history and endeavour. Together, they tell the stories of our nation and the people, places and events that have shaped it.

It is fitting, therefore, that the Library should hold in its collections the work of Australian artist Ellis Rowan. Painting in the late nineteenth and early twentieth centuries, Rowan worked independently, pursuing her vision to comprehensively document the plant life of Australia and the region. In so doing, she became one of Australia's most recognised and prolific artists.

The Flower Hunter: Ellis Rowan is the first exhibition to reveal the art of Ellis Rowan in all its depth and variety. It draws extensively on the Library's own pre-eminent collection of Rowan's works, the majority of which were acquired in 1923, the year after the artist's death. The exhibition includes oil paintings, gouache and watercolour paintings, ceramics and other decorative arts, publications, medals and manuscripts.

The story of Ellis Rowan's life is one of determination and adventure. Through her paintings in this exhibition, and many other examples, which can be viewed through the Library's web site, it is possible to trace her journey from genteel, talented amateur to independent professional artist—an artistic journey matched by a love of travel that took her from Mount Macedon in Victoria across Australia and around the world.

An exhibition such as *The Flower Hunter: Ellis Rowan* is a collaborative event and I would like to thank our guest curator, Patricia Fullerton, who has worked with the staff of the National Library to produce a memorable exhibition, catalogue and online publication. We have also been very fortunate to have the support of a number of public institutions and private lenders. Their collections have enhanced our own and I would like to thank them for their generosity.

Jan Fullerton
Director-General

Chrysanthemums 1888
oil on canvas; 119.5 x 91.5 cm
Winner of First Order of Merit and Gold Medal at the 1888 Centennial International Exhibition, Melbourne Exhibition Building
Private collection, Sydney

CONTENTS

[Ellis Rowan and her son Eric (Puck) Rowan] c.1886
albumen photograph
Private collection

THE FLOWER HUNTER: ELLIS ROWAN
Patricia Fullerton

My love for the flora of Australia, at once so unique and fascinating, together with my desire to complete my collection of floral paintings, has carried me into other colonies, Queensland, and some of the remotest parts of the great Continent of Australia. The excitement of seeking and the delight of finding rare or even unknown specimens abundantly compensated me for all my difficulties, fatigue, and hardships. The pursuit has made me acquainted with many strange phases of colonial life; it has carried me into the depths of jungles, to distant lands, to wild mountain districts, and has brought me into contact with the Aboriginal races, often in peculiar circumstances.[1]

Petite, plucky and always immaculately dressed in the constraint of Victorian finery, for almost 50 years Ellis Rowan explored the world in search of exotic flowers and wildlife to paint. At a time when travel was rough and fraught with danger this intrepid explorer went where few painters had ventured before. From the tropical rainforests of Queensland and remote parts of the Australian outback, her quest took her to New Zealand, the Himalayas, Europe, United States, Caribbean and the high country of Papua New Guinea. Today over 3000 works in major public and private collections testify to her prodigious output and her determination to record as many, until then unknown, specimens: many of which have since become endangered or extinct.

Most of Ellis Rowan's original watercolour studies on grey paper were executed under extreme difficulties: in the heat of the dusty desert, pestered by flies, or in the humid conditions of a tropical rainforest where snakes and crocodiles lurked. She worked quickly and often on site. Her powers of observation, compositional skill, sense of colour, her deftness with the brush and natural facility of technique without any preliminary sketch, were without compromise.

Throughout her life she was acclaimed internationally, winning 29 medals, and accolades from leading art critics, including the ex-President of the British Royal Academy, Lord Leighton. Her work was also collected by royalty, including Queen Victoria. Few painters in the history of Australian art have been so honoured: yet it is hard to think of any who have been so maligned, particularly by male artists, in an ongoing debate on the merit of her work in the 80 years since her death. It is not simply that Ellis Rowan was a woman working in a field dominated by men and reaping rewards that established Australian artists such as Tom Roberts and Julian Ashton felt they more justly deserved. Her subject-matter, drawn from a meticulous observation of nature, isolated her from the landscapists and figure painters of the day. The dilemma in appreciating her work has always been that it falls between two camps; she combined botanical accuracy with an individual style that bordered on the romantic and, later, became boldly dramatic in colour and presentation.

Ellis Rowan belonged to an age when the exacting task of scientific botanical illustration was mostly done by men, and it was considered that dabbling in painting pretty flowers was a woman's foible. However, by the end of the nineteenth century the contribution to botanical knowledge by women was becoming increasingly significant. Rowan was one of these women, but, what set her apart from other female flower painters of the time, was her obsessive commitment, ambition and unabashed self-promotion, as well as her individual style and natural artistic flair. Like many of her contemporaries, her work incorporated the Aesthetic Movement—'Art for Art's

Sake'—a movement that embraced all things decorative, including the painting of screens, murals, designs for porcelain, illustrations for books and magazines, and other creative areas, including writing.

By the age of 50 Ellis Rowan had achieved such recognition in Australia and the international art world that she was already an Australian household name. She was mid-career and in the same year she published her autobiography *A Flower-Hunter in Queensland and New Zealand* (Sydney: Angus and Robertson, 1898) based on entertaining, but factually inaccurate letters to her family. As yet, she had not had a solo exhibition in Europe, nor explored the Americas or the remote parts of Papua New Guinea. Few letters and no diaries remain from her life prior to, or after, the events described in this book: her press cuttings are undated and give little reference to their source. Despite several biographies written since then and well-researched catalogues, many aspects of her extraordinary life and personal details remain a mystery.[2]

Marian Ellis Rowan née Ryan was born in Melbourne on 30 July 1848, the eldest of seven children of pioneering parents, Charles and Marian Ryan. Her father had emigrated from Kilfera, County Kilkenny, Ireland, in 1840, taking a lease at *Kilfera Station*, some 120 kilometres north of Melbourne in the Port Phillip District, then part of the colony of New South Wales.

Her mother was the eldest daughter of the English naturalist and ornithologist, John Cotton, who emigrated with his wife and nine children in 1843, taking up several properties on the Goulburn and Broken Rivers including *Doogallook*, not far from Charles Ryan.[3] Although Ellis Rowan was a baby at the time of her grandfather's death, she inherited his sketchbooks as well as his botanical interest and artistic ability.[4]

By the time of John Cotton's death in 1849, Charles Ryan had already leased *Killeen Station* at Longwood, near the Strathbogie Ranges, where the young Ellis Rowan spent her early childhood. After five years on the land, like many pastoralists at the time, Ryan foresaw that, with the economic changes arising from the gold rush, more money could be made in the city. In 1853 he set up a successful business in Melbourne. There, Ellis Ryan attended Miss Murphy's refined school, taking subjects required for a young Victorian lady: scripture, French, English history, singing, the art of embroidery, lace-making and painting in watercolour.

Unknown photographer
[Miss Ellis Ryan in a Swiss outfit] 1864
albumen photograph; 22.0 x 16.3 cm
Manuscript Collection MS2206

From an early age she was known as Ellis, as much to distinguish her from her mother, Marian, as to pay tribute to her Irish grandmother, Ellis Agar Hartley, the illegitimate child of King George IV and the Countess of Brandon.[5] After her marriage, she developed the stylised vertical signature 'Ellis Rowan' into her flower paintings, making it integral to the branches and leaves, almost like the camouflage of a stick insect. It was this distinctive signature that first aroused the curiosity of her biographer, Margaret Hazzard, who, some 60 years after her death, wanted to learn more of this 'unknown male artist'.[6]

In 1869, aged 21, Rowan made her first trip abroad, basing herself in England for a year. Although it has been said that she made this visit to England 'with the intention of taking lessons in painting', she later denied it.[7] In one of her many interviews, in which she often contradicted herself, she claimed that she was told to 'develop her talents along the lines she had been working on, and continue to work steadily from Nature rather than change to formal landscape or portraiture'.[8] Her uncle was the Royal Academician, Sir Charles Eastlake, so she would have had every opportunity to avail herself of London's artistic circles. Whether she took lessons or not, it is clear that she had been busy honing her skills in the fashionable pastime for young Victorian ladies of flower painting, for on her return, 'Miss Ellis Ryan' won a bronze medal for a screen, with four panels of Australian wildflowers at the Intercolonial Exhibition Melbourne in 1872.

Whatever her botanical interests had been, they would have expanded when her father, a keen botanist himself, bought 26 acres on Mount Macedon and built what was to become, for both him and Rowan, their favourite home and final resting place. *Derriweit Heights* commanded one of the best views on the Mount. It was a typical colonial hill-station, built on the south-west slope, near the historic site where Surveyor-General Major Mitchell had declared the rich pastoral plain below as 'Australia Felix' in 1836. It was acclaimed to be one of the finest homes in the nation and the garden became internationally famous, particularly for botanists and horticulturists. Ferdinand von Mueller, the government botanist, advised on exotic plants from around the world, and the garden layout was designed by W.R. Guilfoyle.

The house looked down over a sloping lawn, where Guilfoyle used a mountain stream to create five lakes. Covered in waterlilies and bordered by ferns, clumps of New Zealand flax, with groves of silver birches and Japanese maples to provide dappled shade, the lakes became one of the great features of *Derriweit Heights*. Rhododendrons were planted under exotic trees, as well as foxgloves, violets and gentians along the shady paths that led from one level of the garden to another, creating a series of 'bosky dells' and colourful displays set against the Australian bush background, where koalas and platypus abounded.[9]

Through her father's collaboration with von Mueller in the choice of plants for the garden, Rowan was invited to contribute botanical studies for his comprehensive collection on Australian flora. Ferdinand von Mueller had come to Australia seeking new medicinal plants to escape from the deadly pattern of tuberculosis in his family and took up the position of Director of the Royal Botanical Gardens in Melbourne. He enlisted a team of artists from around the continent to contribute to his encyclopaedic knowledge of indigenous flora, in anticipation of a publication on the subject.[10] It is not known precisely when Rowan started submitting her works to him, but von Mueller's bold handwriting appears on the back of many of her pictures identifying the subjects in botanical Latin. 'The Baron', as he was known after receiving the title from King Wurtemburg of Prussia in 1861, encouraged her work and gave her useful introductions to key people around the world. They kept in touch until his death in 1896.

In June 1873 Ellis Ryan, now a captivating 25-year-old and equipped with artistic ability and skills for marriage, became engaged to Captain Frederic Charles Rowan, an officer in the British army. Frederic Rowan had spent several years in England undergoing facial reconstruction after being wounded in the New Zealand Maori Wars, before returning via Melbourne to become Sub-Inspector for the Constabulary of Armed Forces in New Zealand. Four months after meeting

J. Botterill, Portrait Painter and Photographer
[Ellis Rowan in her wedding dress] 1873
albumen photograph; 14.4 x 10.2 cm
Manuscript Collection MS2206

they celebrated their marriage at the Ryan family home in Richmond, before settling in New Zealand at Pukearuhe on the North Island. Living as an officer's wife, isolated from friends and family, Rowan found the domesticity of married life 'boring'; but, ever resourceful, and under her husband's exacting eye and encouragement, she applied herself to painting local wildflowers. Many years later she recalled these early days of marriage:

> From having as a girl lived a life full of gaiety, I was suddenly cut off from all social pleasures and for the first time I was thrown entirely on my own resources; yet these solitudes in which for months at a time we never saw a strange face, are among the very happiest of my recollections, and here for the first time I commenced … getting as good a collection of the Australasian flora as I could.[11]

Years later in New York she recalled: 'Long into the night, longing to give up, to give in, sometimes with tears running down my face, I worked to please him'.[12] Despite her ostensible altruism in painting flowers, she confessed in her autobiography: 'The task which I undertook at first to please him, soon became my greatest interest and unfailing source of pleasure.'[13]

In January 1875 Ellis Rowan left her husband in New Zealand, returning to her family home in Macedon where she painted for six months awaiting the birth of her only child, Frederic Charles Eric Elliott Rowan, known simply as Puck. They spent the next three years in New Zealand before Frederic Rowan returned to Australia in 1878 to establish himself and his family in the thriving business world of Melbourne, the most prosperous city in Australasia. 'Marvellous Melbourne' was the catch-cry of the day and Frederic Rowan, an astute businessman interested in new technology, was one of many to profit from the booming economy. Through his influential connections he was able to assist his wife's career: he was a member of the board of *The Picturesque Atlas of Australasia*, which, in 1886, published illustrations by Ellis Rowan and other known artists.[14] As the corporate wife, Rowan accompanied her husband on his energetic business trips around Australia, taking the opportunity to paint indigenous flowers wherever she could. On her initial trips to Adelaide and Western Australia, she painted delicate bouquets of mixed wildflowers, which she exhibited for the first time under her married name, 'Mrs F.C. Rowan', at the Sydney International Exhibition in 1879, winning a silver medal.

In October 1880 the Melbourne Exhibition Building opened in style, attracting exhibits from 30 countries and the six Australian colonies, with 32,000 samples of produce and culture. Here Rowan first incurred the indignation of her fellow painters when she won a gold medal for a four-leaved screen on satin and special merit for ten framed groups of New Zealand wildflowers on satin.[15] Rowan and another flower painter, Catherine Purves, were the only artists

[*Orchids—Common Spider Orchid (Caladenia patersonii),*
Blue China Orchid (Caladenia gemmata), Pink Fairies
(Caladenia latifolia), Common Donkey Orchid (Diuris
longifolia)] 1880
Western Australia
gouache and watercolour on paper; 54.8 x 38.0 cm
nla.pic–an6730524 Pictures Collection R2132

Australia. The daughter of British politician, Frederick North, she was well connected and of independent means. Although there is no official record, North may have encouraged Rowan in the technique of oil painting and given her ideas about placing flowers in their natural habitat to show surrounding vegetation in a landscape background with atmospheric effects such as a brooding storm or a setting sun. Like many botanical painters at the time, she was inspired by Thornton's famous florilegium *The Temple of Flora*, which encouraged artists to travel and depict exotic flora in Arcadian settings, instead of academic illustrations showing root structure, seeds, leaves and flowers on a plain background.[16] North included birds, butterflies, fungi and insects in her paintings, as much for their intrinsic interest as to show their role in the ecological balance of nature. She inspired Rowan with ideas of freedom to travel wherever and whenever she could, not to mention ideas about writing of her adventures and also of how to house and promote her works for posterity. Twenty-five years later Rowan recalled:

> I became her devoted admirer, and she became the pioneer of my ambition. A world-wide traveller in search of specimens, her description of her adventures was so vivid, so graphic, so thrilling in its prospects of wider fields that I became infected, stimulated by an example and a result beyond dreams successful … I resolved to do as she had done. I would travel the world in search of flowers rare and wonderful, travel countries inaccessible, as well as those which offered difficulties only imaginary.[17]

Twenty years older, and renowned for her shabby attire, North was equally fascinated by Rowan. Not only did she later visit Rowan at Mount Macedon, but she recorded their meeting in Albany and Rowan's approach to painting in her diary:

> The difficulty was to choose the flowers. One was tempted to bring home so many, and as they were mostly very small and delicate, it was not possible to paint half of them. Mrs Rowan did it most exquisitely in a peculiar way of her own on gray

awarded gold medals in the art section. Members of the Victorian Artists' Society protested to the jurors, who stuck by their decision, but later, begrudgingly, conceded a silver medal to Louis Buvelot, the highly esteemed painter of the Australian landscape. Rowan ignored the petty squabblings and competitive jealousy of the art world and set about discovering new flowers to paint for von Mueller.

On one of her many trips with her husband, in 1880, Rowan met the lone English painter, Marianne North, at Albany on the south coast of Western

paper. She was a very pretty fairy-like little woman, always over-dressed, and afraid to go out of the house because people stared at her. I admired her for her genius and prettiness; she was like a charming spoiled child. [18]

Peince, Photographer
[Ellis Rowan sketching in the garden at *Derriweit Heights* with her son Puck on his pony and Mary Moule reading] 1887
albumen photograph; 19.3 x 24.0 cm

In March 1883, leaving her husband and eight-year-old son, and armed with introductions, Rowan and her sister Blanche Ryan travelled to England via Ceylon and India, where she painted in the Himalayan foothills. At the Intercolonial Exhibition in Calcutta her works were compared with the new art form of photography: 'There are a dozen watercolours in the Victorian Court, of the indigenous wildflowers of Australia … which in point of excellence, of execution, beauty of colouring and artistic grouping … are worth all the photographs in the exhibition put together'.[19] That year Rowan won gold medals in Amsterdam, St Petersburg and Calcutta, and the following year one for lace-making in Denmark, shortly after her husband had been appointed Danish consul in Melbourne.

The 1880s was a highly productive decade for Ellis Rowan: not only did she paint a number of rare species for von Mueller's classification but, with a growing sense of commercialism encouraged by her husband, she made several versions of her more popular subjects on green paper for sale in exhibitions and to keep for her own record. She also learned the delicate art of engraving: over 100 engravings of her flowers and scenes were published in *Australasia Illustrated* in 1887.[20] It may have been due to this refined new medium, as well as to her newfound confidence after meeting Marianne North, that from this time her watercolours, now beginning to incorporate landscape and insects, became bolder in colour and presentation, and she started to paint in oils.

By the winter of 1887, Rowan made the first of six trips to Queensland. Overwhelmed by the luscious colour and succulence of the tropical vegetation, she did some of her best paintings in dazzling colour and startling composition, which were duly recognised the following year.

She was 40 years old when she again upset her fellow painters and caused a major stir in Australia's art world by scooping the awards at the 1888 Centennial International Exhibition. With pomp and ceremony the exhibition at the Melbourne Exhibition Building was staged as the grandest show of its kind yet held. Opened by the Governor Sir Henry Loch, it included every country in the British Empire as well as Europe, America and Japan. Most known Australian artists had an eye on the painting prize, including Frederick McCubbin, John Mather, Arthur Loureiro, Tom Roberts and George Ashton. For the first time Rowan exhibited as 'Mrs Ellis Rowan'.

Out of all the entries, both local and foreign, the jury of 15 internationally respected connoisseurs singled out Victoria, Queensland and New Zealand, as having the most interesting works: 'but if we except the flower paintings of Mrs Rowan, none of the works exhibited are of sufficient importance to call for special comment … Her masterly delineations of the

Faradaya splendida [*Buku*] c.1887
Queensland
gouache and watercolour on paper; 54.7 x 38.0 cm
nla.pic–an6723103 Pictures Collection R2618

Australian and New Zealand flowers … have secured for her the highest honour.' Again, eight years after her previous success at the Exhibition Buildings, she won top awards:

> *Mrs Ellis Rowan, First Order of Merit and a Gold Medal for her picture* Chrysanthemums, *and a collection of 17 flower pieces in the Victorian court, also an unspecified number in the Queensland court, 24 pictures in New Zealand court.*
> *Second Prize Mrs Rowan for her picture* Marguerites.
> *Second Prize: Tom Roberts, three oil paintings:* Reconciliation, Blue Eyes and Brown, C.S. Patterson.
> *Third Prize: Fred McCubbin and John Mather.* [21]

Both her winning works, *Chrysanthemums* and *Marguerites*, were large competent oil paintings, a medium in which she had not exhibited before: thus, in the eyes of the judges, earning extra merit for their originality. There was a storm of protest. Her male colleagues were angry: not only was she a woman, but a mere flower painter at that. Members of the Victorian Artists' Society called a meeting to contest the judgement, as they had done eight years before. Their indignant letter concluded: 'the one first-class award made to Australian art is a direct insult to the foreign artists who have done Australia the honour of competing in its International Exhibition'. Not only did the jury confirm their decision, but they ridiculed the insolence of the Society and the signatories, John Mather and George Ashton, questioning which was more offensive: 'The ludicrous attempt to protect and patronise the foreign artists, or the cruel and unmanly effort to injure the artistic reputation of the lady overtly referred to in the resolution.'[22] Although this was a major triumph for Rowan, the bitterness of her male rivals was permanent and they continued to spurn and ridicule her work long after her death, contributing to the difficulty of later finding a lasting home for her paintings.[23]

Ellis Rowan was now the most recognised painter in Australia and was rapidly becoming a household name. The following year in 1889, she went on to win five first prizes and a gold medal at the Adelaide Jubilee Exhibition and her success, as well as her social connections, led to commissions in oils. She painted murals at her cousin Lady Janet Clarke's house *Cliveden*, murals in the governor's dining room at the Victorian Racing Club and, even more unlikely for a woman at the time, in 1893, she painted 12 large oil panels for the walls of The Australian Club, the prestigious men's club in Melbourne.[24]

During this time she also kept up her travels, visiting Western Australia in September 1889 for a painting tour with her flower-painting friend, Margaret Forrest. They went to Boolantha Station, north of Carnarvon and Geraldton, to sketch desert spring flowers. Their joint showing at the Railway Station Reading Room in Perth on 5 November, was said to be the first art exhibition ever held in the colony, with 'some of the loveliest flowers ever seen'.[25]

Rowan returned to the tropical warmth of Queensland during the winters of 1891 and 1892, claiming a need to escape for her health. She took Puck with her for a few weeks on the first trip. Captivated by the variety of the lush tropical vegetation, she sent 65 paintings back to von Mueller for identification. According to the records of these trips she visited Normanby, Rockhampton, Mount Morgan, Mackay, Thursday Island, Cape York, Cooktown, Somerset, Murray Island, Jervis Island, Cairns, Hambledon, Muldiva, Chillagoe Caves, Barron Falls, Myola and Herberton.[26] The exaggerated letters describing her adventures to her husband Frederic Rowan form the first part of her autobiography:

> *My first walk in the wild tropical jungle … I cannot forget. I entered, sketchbook in hand, by a narrow little pathway, probably made by an alligator. I kicked, as I thought, a grey stick aside—it was a snake, and quick as lightning it darted off, while I grew hot and cold in turns … A few steps farther on I came to an opening, and below me lay a miniature lake, its water covered with large blue lilies floating amid their leaves on which the sun shone through a network of graceful palms.*

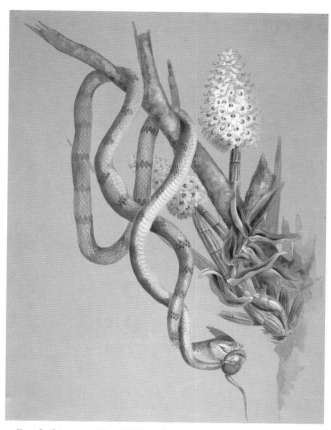

Dendrobium smillieae [*White-flowered variety and Brown Tree Snake 'with a bird just caught between its jaws'*] 1887
Mackay, Queensland
gouache and watercolour on paper; 54.7 x 38.0 cm
nla.pic–an6731158 Pictures Collection R2195

Scarlet, yellow-eyed dragonflies skimmed over its surface, while presently a great butterfly tremulously fluttered past, and the sunlight, catching the metallic lustre of its wings, changed them to every rainbow hue.[27]

So began her account of her fascination for the exotic plant and insect life of tropical Queensland. Her vivid descriptions reveal the eye of an artist, while her tales of near disaster fully satisfied her lust for adventure. She suffered bruises, a black eye and the occasional fever, complained of stinging nettles, mosquito bites and sunburn. Amongst other things in her quest, she dangled by ropes over precipices, defied turbulent seas, a bolting horse and a hair-raising trip by rail.

While she marvelled at the vegetation and wildlife, she was less than complimentary about the Indigenous people, describing them with typical colonial condescension of the time, as lazy, ugly and dangerous: 'The natives are not very civilised here, and a few days ago killed and ate a Chinaman; they seem to have an aversion to (or perhaps I should say a fancy for) this particular race.'[28] She also asserted with some authority, that cannibalism caused 'piebald' pigmentation to their skin, and claimed that she was one of the first white women to witness a corroboree and sexual rituals: 'They generally, in their love-making, seize upon and carry off their wives, if from another tribe, the young "Lochinvar" generally commences operations by stunning her on the head to prevent her from screaming: this generally is an excuse for declaring war, which is a sort of pastime to them.'[29]

Her return to Melbourne in December 1892 coincided with her husband's sudden death at 47, two days later, thought to be from pneumonia. Although they had spent much of their life apart, Frederic Rowan had fully supported her career throughout their marriage. Their relationship was not close in the conventional sense, but they had shared an intimacy in their letters and expectations of each other. The young widow, now in her mid-forties, dressed appropriately in black, made her home permanently at *Derriweit Heights*.[30] After a short period of grieving, Rowan began her travels again with a new sense of freedom, revisiting New Zealand the following year on a lengthy trip covering both the North and South Islands. During her travels she painted black and white landscapes which were reproduced in *The Town and Country Journal* in December 1893, with a serialised account of her trip. Her adventure-packed letters to her family form the second part of her autobiography. That same year, in 1893, she entered what was to be her last international competition, exhibiting 99 paintings in the World Columbian Exhibition in Chicago, celebrating the 400 years since Christopher Columbus discovered America. She won a gold medal.[31] Now with a total of 29 medals (ten gold, 15 silver and four bronze), she confined her exhibiting to solo shows, where her works could be sold.

In 1895 Ellis Rowan embarked on a trip to England which was to take her away from Australia for some ten years. Through the connections of her younger brother Cecil Ryan and armed with a large number of paintings, Rowan made contact with royalty and, briefly, the elderly Queen Victoria herself. Asked to leave her pictures behind Rowan received a letter from Windsor Castle within days of her visit: 'The Queen has seen your paintings and … was much pleased with them … [and] has kept three. These the Queen will have made into a screen for her own room and there they will prove not only most ornamental but most useful to Her Majesty.'[32]

The following year, in 1896, Ellis Rowan staged her first solo show outside Australia, exhibiting 100 paintings of Australian wildflowers at the fashionable Dowdeswell Galleries in New Bond Street, Mayfair. At the private viewing on 20 April 1896, the Queen's cousin, the Duchess of Teck, opened the show and bought three paintings for herself. The papers were filled with descriptions of the glittering occasion and many glowing reviews, including one by the eminent ex-President of the Royal Academy, Lord Leighton: 'Mrs Rowan's work is characterised by exquisite purity of tone without feebleness, and the most brilliant colour without harshness—each specimen botanically perfect … created into a lovely picture'.[33] The following month in 'The Art Notes' of *The Sketch*, an article arguing as to whether the nation should acquire Lord Leighton's assets since his recent death, coincided with a warm review of Rowan's exhibition, which concluded: 'The only objection we have is to the names of these wildflowers; it is to us little short of extraordinary that Mrs Rowan can be on terms of familiarity with a "Limnanthemum-exaltatumutricularia-didotomo-labillandra".'[34]

For the first time since the discovery of gold and infamous reports on convicts or Ned Kelly, the major Australian topic of interest in London was its wildflowers. Not only had Ellis Rowan become a good ambassador for her country, but she sold well, resulting in commissions for murals and oil paintings in prestigious addresses around London, including 13 panels for Lord Newton's house in Belgrave Square.[35]

Her friendship with von Mueller led to a meeting with the German Chancellor, Prince von Bismarck, whom she claimed offered to purchase her collection for £15,000 and who invited her to remain in Germany as its botanical artist: an offer she refused on the grounds of patriotism, apparently preferring her works to remain in Australia.[36] Instead, she set her sights on America. Equipped with introductions, she set off for a visit which lasted more than seven years. In New York, she met the young botanist Alice Lounsberry and together, over four years, they travelled through the United States and the West Indies, collaborating on three books which became standard texts for botany students: *A Guide to the Wildflowers* (1899), *A Guide to the Trees* (1900), and *Southern Wildflowers and Trees* (1901).[37]

Except for some hyperbolic interviews in the newspapers, her years in the United States are probably the least documented of her life. After completing her work with Lounsberry, she continued to travel and paint throughout the States. She held several exhibitions at prestigious venues, including The Field Columbian Museum in Chicago and Clausen's Gallery, Fifth Ave, New York, where 500 paintings of her wildflowers of the United States, the West Indies, Australia and New Zealand were shown. In 1904 she travelled to the Mexican border, across the Sierras to California for the Panama-Pacific Exposition at Stanford University. In spite of a later claim that she wanted her works to remain in Australia, during her stay she made many attempts to find a permanent home for her collection in America.

It was during the first months of this visit that she learned of the deaths of her father and also of her son Puck, who died tragically aged 22 in a gaol in Mashonaland, Zimbabwe, where he may have been involved with the Australian cavalry during the Boer War.[38] Sometime after hearing the news, she underwent a transformation with experimental surgery on her face. This 'face-lift', a new American fad, gave her, what one reporter described as, 'the look of a sad monkey in a small childish face'.[39] Whether for reasons of vanity or to expel the ravages of grief from her face, exacerbated by many years spent in the harsh Australian sun, or possibly to compete with Alice Lounsberry, who was 25 years younger, or maybe inspired by her husband's facial reconstruction before their marriage; she not only changed her face, but dyed her hair red with henna, and also reduced her said-age by ten years. In *The American Botanical and Historical Record* she mentioned her marriage date, but made no mention of a son and quoted her birth-date as 1858.

It is not known precisely, but records suggest Rowan came back to Melbourne towards the end of 1904, as she stayed with her cousin Lady Janet Clarke at *Cliveden* and the following year joined the landscape classes of her former rival John Mather. In 1906 she visited Perth and once again turned to the remote and inhospitable parts of Australia as a focus for her work, making a foray north-east to the goldmining area of Kalgoorlie, Laverton and Goongarrie. Despite her incongruous appearance, dressed in long white skirt, nipped in at the waist by a sash, with gloves and veil, the local people regarded her with respect, bringing her flowers to paint and, on one occasion, presenting her with a baby bilby or bandicoot rabbit, which she called Bill Baillie.

At the Australian Natives' Association Hall in Kalgoorlie she held a successful exhibition including 20 landscapes of the goldmining region (some of which she later used to illustrate her book *Bill Baillie*[40]) and 130 desert flower paintings, including kangaroo paws, orchids, banksias and the coral creeper. Again she claimed her passion for Western Australian flora, stating that some of the most beautiful flowers were found in the sand-hills near Laverton, some 500 kilometres north of Kalgoorlie. On return to Perth however, she was disappointed when these same paintings, so widely praised in her desert show, were disregarded at an Australian Exhibition of Women's Work in Hay Street on the grounds that she was not a local artist. She later said: 'In Western Australia they simply refused to look at my exhibition because so many of the ladies over there paint wildflowers themselves'.[41]

Although Ellis Rowan was looking for a major buyer for her entire collection, a number of key purchases of her works were made during this time. The South Australian Government bought 80 works for £500 from a much acclaimed Adelaide exhibition.[42] Some of these were a collection of wildflower paintings from a trip Rowan made to Broken Hill in time to capture a rich red carpet of Sturt's Desert peas in full bloom. Sir John Downer, the politician and supporter of women's rights, who had been a colleague of Rowan's husband, bought 20 works. These were bequeathed to the State government in 1918, following the death of his brother George. Transferred to the Museum of South Australia in 1940, these paintings are today housed in the

[Ellis Rowan with her mother Marian Ryan, and sisters Mabel and Blanche Ryan in the garden at *Derriweit Heights*, Mount Macedon] c.1885
albumen photograph
Private collection

Cup and saucer with waratah design 1916–1918
hand painted porcelain; cup 5.0 cm height, 11.0 cm width (includes handle); saucer 2.0 cm height, 12.2 cm diameter
Courtesy of the Powerhouse Museum, Sydney

South Australian Herbarium at the Botanical Gardens in Adelaide. On return to Melbourne she held several successful shows and later that year, from her exhibition at the Angus and Robertson Gallery in Sydney, the Sydney Technical College bought 65 paintings, which are housed today in the Powerhouse Museum.

In 1909, shortly after her exhibition at the Scourfield Galleries in Melbourne, the anthropologist and collector, Sir Baldwin Spencer suggested building a museum to house her collection, in the way Marianne North had done in Kew.[43] Unlike North's oil paintings, Rowan's works could never be permanently on display, since watercolours deteriorate with exposure. Besides, the sheer quantity of more than 1000 works would have been impossible to hang at any given time. Today, in her home town Melbourne, Rowan is represented by

five works in the National Gallery of Victoria, one of which, *Pandorea jasminoides*, is rated a public favourite in the collection.

The Queensland State Government botanist Frederick Manson Bailley chose 16 of her paintings as colour plates for his *Comprehensive Catalogue of Queensland Plants* (1913), and also named a large spotted orchid in her honour.[44] After her exhibition at the Old Town Hall in Brisbane in August 1912, the Queensland Government bought 100 paintings for £1000. Rowan gave an extra 25 works for £50, making a total of 125 works, which today are housed in the Queensland Museum. The political groundwork that Rowan had put into securing this deal was widely publicised in the press and opened up the debate as to whether her works should be represented as art in a gallery or as botanical studies in a museum. While Rowan was finally beginning to find permanent homes for some of her work, her battle for securing her major collection for posterity was yet to come.

Since returning to Australia Rowan had developed a particular interest in the protection of birds, some of which had become endangered by the current fashion of plumaged hats and feather boas. For some time she had been practising the delicate art of china painting for the Sydney jeweller and importer of fine china, Flavelle Brothers, who sent her designs of waratah, flannel flowers, gum blossom and other Australian flora to the Royal Worcester Porcelain Company in England for copying. They commissioned her to paint 100 flowers and some birds of paradise in Papua New Guinea, an offer she accepted unconditionally. Since her early contact with von Mueller, Rowan had wanted to visit New Guinea, but her husband and others had rightly cautioned her of its danger. After many years of German occupation, in 1914 the Melanesian Islands had become an Australian protectorate: this was her great chance.

In May 1916 and in the middle of the Great War, Ellis Rowan, now 68 years old, set off to Papua New Guinea for seven months, again equipped with an excellent set of connections. On the way she painted some birds of paradise, but the flower paintings from this trip were nothing like the delicate posies of her youth—they had become overwhelmingly luscious, oozing off the edge of the paper, and confrontingly bold in colour.

When she returned to Sydney, welcomed back like a national treasure, Rowan told reporters flocking to interview her, that she had every intention of returning to New Guinea: 'I may say the natives inland are very hostile. It was not however necessary for me to go very far inland. I found the most marvellous flowers quite close at hand, the most wonderful flowers in the whole world—and others were brought to me by the natives. I am the first person to paint these flowers—the first white person indeed to see any of them. I need not, therefore, say that they have never been classified in a

botanical sense.'[45] One of the flowers she described was the rare Titan Arum, a plant that blooms infrequently.[46] Painted clumsily in liverish browns, the work reflects her nauseous reaction:

> *Some of the flowers are 24 or 30 inches long, but perhaps the most remarkable—not the most beautiful … is one which is circular in shape, and about 15 inches in diameter. It is dark brown and velvety in appearance, and has a thick, fleshy substance under the actual flower, which seems to be in a state of putrefaction. It has a terrible smell—sufficient to poison a whole regiment—but the strange thing is you only smell it between 4 o'clock in the afternoon and 9 o'clock at night.* [47]

In Rowan's successful exhibition at the Technical College in Harris Street, Sydney, in November 1916, her bird of paradise paintings, which were for sale as a collection only, found no buyer, but her flowers on circular maroon-bordered paper, intended for dessert plates by Flavelle Brothers for the Royal Worcester Porcelain Company, were bought by the Kew Gardens Herbarium in London.

The following year in 1917, Rowan returned to New Guinea, this time in an attempt to paint every single bird of paradise, of which 52 were already known. She stayed at the Madang Mission House, on the north coast. The area was dotted with efficient German copra plantations and mission stations, where trade in birds and butterflies was rampant. Since her friendship with von Mueller and her visit to Germany, Rowan had sufficient language skills to arrange an exhibition at a local German store, while awaiting travel to the high country, where the brilliantly plumed birds abounded. Reluctant to send an elderly white woman alone to these dangerous parts, the resident missionary eventually made arrangements for her to be carried in a hammock by a party of guides draped in loin cloths. In the manner that most dealers in plumes operated at the time, the first six birds were brought to her dead. With no intention of painting dead birds, she encouraged the local headhunters, with bribes of tobacco, to deliver them live and housed in cages:

The large ones I tucked under my arm and held in that way while I painted them. Some were fierce and hard to hold ... I covered the heads of others with handkerchiefs or a table napkin to keep them a little quieter while I was painting the body ... Painting the birds and flowers of New Guinea really did mean a mustering up of courage, and searching for the Birds of Paradise led me into all sorts of out-of-the-way places where I saw natives in their primitive state and camped in their villages. But as they said I was tapu *... no-one touched me.*[48]

[**Brown Sickle-billed Bird of Paradise (Epimachus meyeri)**] c.1917
gouache and watercolour on muslin; 16.2 cm diameter
nla.pic–an23712209 Pictures Collection R2683

Living under the most primitive conditions in the tropical heat, inevitably her health broke down and, suffering from malaria and fatigue, she was carried by guides down from the high country to the coast where she was expected to die. With the courage that had seen her through so many intrepid adventures, she rallied and, on return to Australia with over 300 paintings, she went to Macedon to be nursed by her sister Blanche Ryan.

Until recently we have been led to believe that she painted 47 of the known birds from life. However, two letters, in her near-indecipherable handwriting, have

been located in the archives of the Victorian Museum, in which she wrote to the director, Sir Baldwin Spencer, that she had just 'painted 25 birds of paradise in New Guinea' and that she now needed to paint from the stuffed birds in cases at the museum, to help complete her mission.[49] It is not known which birds she painted from life, but she must have painted a further 22 from museum specimens, thus explaining why many of her subjects appear so wooden and lifeless.

Her feat in capturing some 25 live birds was remarkable, but Rowan was not one to go public on this number, and the press was none the wiser when the collection was shown for the first time in Melbourne at the Fine Art Society's Galleries in November 1918. Rowan exhibited 189 paintings: 172 flowers, 40 birds of paradise, 72 fungi, two pictures of coral, a bat, a squirrel and a fish. The *Sun* critic wrote: 'She went to New Guinea with a keen desire to paint the brilliant birds of paradise from life. Hitherto even such notable naturalists as J. Gould, who made a special study of Australian birds, have been content to sketch ... from dead specimens'. The writer perceptively noted: 'The artist is proud of her mushroom collection, only one of her specimens being known to science.' Rowan's description of her rare collection of crinoline fungi sums up their extraordinary fragility: 'Growing, they look like dolls dressed up in fluted lace petticoats ... Some are apple green, others mauve; one is black, and another has a scarlet cap. They stand high on long white stems, and the fungus closely resembles exquisite lace.'[50]

It was after the Melbourne opening at the Fine Art Society's Galleries that the idea of her works being collected by the National Library of Australia was first mooted. In an impassioned letter on the future of an Ellis Rowan collection, the Speaker of the House of Representatives, Elliot Johnson, a friend who was also on the board of the proposed Library, argued its significance to Australia:

it would be a national calamity if the collection were to be disposed of outside Australia ... It has however, come to my

Despite this plea from a man of influence, no financial supporters came forward. Soon after, however, an exhibition was arranged to travel to the United States under the supervision of the entrepreneur, George Meudell.[52] Consisting of 376 paintings of American and West Indian flowers and 280 New Guinea and north Queensland birds and flowers, the show toured to Stanford University, California and then via several other venues onto New York. There it was noted:

A unique series of watercolours of birds of paradise is on view [at] the American Museum of Natural History. The artist is Mrs Ellis Rowan who is so well known through her paintings of flowers of the West Indies and her very complete series comprising 300 illustrations of the gorgeous native flowers of Australia and adjacent islands.[53]

Although Meudell found no major philanthropist to purchase the collection, several paintings from the exhibition were sold to individual American buyers.[54]

In her final years, still campaigning for her works to become a national collection, and suffering from the effects of malaria, Rowan continued her designs for the Royal Worcester Porcelain Company, receiving accolades for her birds of paradise which were copied by Sedgeley and Phillips and the Austin brothers.[55] Unstoppable, she turned her attention to painting a series of butterflies from the famous Dodd collection,

which she probably first saw when she visited Kuranda in 1911, and most likely again in 1917, when she sailed with the Dodds on the *Morinda* to New Guinea.[56] F.P. Dodd, had collected a vast number of rare, tropical butterflies and insects which he traded to wealthy patrons, including Lord Rothschild, when it was fashionable in certain circles to have private entomological drawers for display.

These intricate paintings of tropical butterflies and insects, copied from the artistically arranged cases of Dodd, are among Rowan's greatest achievements. Arranged in serried ranks by the professional

[*Netted Stinkhorn Fungus, Dictyophora phalloidea or Dictyophora multicolor*]
c.1916–1917
Papua New Guinea
gouache and watercolour on paper; 28.0 x 19.0 cm
From the Collection of Anna Macgowan

Freycinetia marginata [*Pandanus*] *with Brown Butterfly* [*Nymphalidae satyridae*]

c.1916–1917

Papua New Guinea

gouache and watercolour on paper; 75.8 x 56.1 cm

nla.pic–an23621188 Pictures Collection R1780

lepidopterist himself, in a *trompe l'oeil* effect, Rowan has captured the essence of each insect as if caught in nature. Exhibited in her 1920 show at Horderns, these butterflies have scarcely been recorded since.[57]

From her cousin Una Falkiner's Riverina property, *Widgiewa*, where she spent her last winters, Rowan wrote: 'I have just finished 2175 butterflies and moths of New Guinea, that means work, as they are difficult to paint.'[58] While a great-niece recalled a visit to Rowan's attic at the Macedon Cottage: 'There were sheets of paper leaning against the wall at the back of the shelf with rows and rows of butterflies painted on them, it was hard for me to realise that she had actually done the painting herself.'[59]

In March 1920 Ellis Rowan made what would be a final gesture to the Australian public when she staged the largest solo exhibition yet held in the country, displaying 1000 paintings, including her butterflies, at Anthony Hordern's Gallery in Sydney. Except for her birds of paradise, all works were for sale, ranging from ten to 125 guineas. The sales of the exhibition amounted to over £2000, making a record for a woman artist at the time.[60] Opened by Governor Sir Walter Davidson, he urged that the collection be bought by the nation, a point reiterated the following day in an article entitled 'A Rare Collection': 'it is exceedingly important that the works of Mrs Rowan should be preserved as a national collection, for their educative value is very great indeed. The New Guinea collection on show … is an amazing achievement for any woman to have accomplished.'[61]

Until the day she died Rowan doggedly campaigned for her collection to be bought for the Australian public and the destiny of her works became a major topic on the floor of Parliament House as well as in letters to the press. The politician, Dr Earle Page, declared paintings of flowers were not 'a very high form of art' and that if the government were to purchase a series of pictures of the flora and fauna of Australia he would prefer 'faithful and effective photographic reproductions'.[62] Many were unconditional in their support, but the carping bitterness of her male rivals continued. One critic said her work was 'undistinguished', and the painter of nudes, Norman Lindsay, whose taste has long been questionable, wrote with some irony, that her paintings were 'vulgar'.[63] To give him some credit, he may have been speaking of her later New Guinean flowers, which bleed off the page in such bold colour and profusion that might have made the American modernist, Georgia O'Keefe, proud. Although her work was uneven, and she may be fairly criticised for repeating many of her better-selling subjects, Ellis Rowan painted more species of Australian and international flora than any other artist of her era and, at her best, produced some of the most powerfully arresting flower paintings recorded in Australian art.

A public campaign was organised by the Rowan Collection Committee which attracted some notable and influential supporters: Prime Minister, Billy Hughes, Director of the then National Gallery of New South Wales, G.V.F. Mann, eminent portraitist John Longstaff, Professor A.A. Lawson, foundation Professor of Botany at the University of Sydney, and the painter Will Ashton. They unanimously agreed that the collection had 'great historical, artistic, educational and scientific value', adding that it was unique and could not be repeated 'due to the peculiar temperament and circumstances of the Artist … [which] rarely occur in one personality'. They also referred to its value for the arts and crafts movement of the time, claiming it as a source of inspiration for Australian wallpaper, friezes, as well as china and pottery painting.[64]

With the future of her life's work still unresolved, Ellis Rowan died at Macedon on 4 October 1922. Her death certificate declared 'heart failure, pulmonary congestion/pleurisy'. Tributes from around Australia poured in to the press: 'To those fortunate to meet her, the painter was more wonderful than her work—and that is saying a great deal. The first impression was of a fiery, intense vitality in a seemingly most fragile personality. Her conversation was brilliant, full of crisp descriptions of people and places … She had a power of endurance which strong men might envy ... and worked as if upheld by some power greater than any inherent in human flesh and blood.'[65] She is buried at the foothills of her beloved Mount Macedon in a family grave with her parents and sisters Blanche and Mabel Ryan, her great-nephew Patrick and his wife, Rosemary Ryan, and nearby her niece, Maie Casey and husband Richard, Baron Casey of Berwick.

The year after her death, the Commonwealth Government finally purchased 947 of her watercolours for £5000, thought to be a meagre sum for her sister Blanche, who was the sole survivor and executrix. These works, housed since then in the collection of the National Library of Australia, are the source and inspiration from which this exhibition is largely drawn.

Twenty–two butterflies all belonging to the family Nymphalidae, including *Vindula arsinoe, Cethosia cydippe, Parthenos aspila,* and five species of *Hypolimnas* c.1918–1920
watercolour and gouache on paper; 56.2 x 33.7 cm
Private collection

NOTES

1 Preface to Ellis Rowan, *A Flower-Hunter in Queensland and New Zealand*. Sydney: Angus and Robertson, 1898. The first part of the autobiography was based on letters to her family and husband from her three trips to Queensland in 1887, 1889 and 1892. The second part is based on her trip to New Zealand in 1893, most of which was serialised in *The Town and Country* in December 1893, with black and white illustrations of scenes in New Zealand. Rowan's autobiography was reprinted as *The Flower Hunter: The Adventures in Northern Australia and New Zealand of Flower Painter Ellis Rowan* (Sydney: Angus and Robertson/HarperCollins, 1991). References to Rowan's autobiography made in this catalogue come from the 1991 reprint.

2 A fire at the Ryan's Macedon home *Derriweit Heights* in 1898 may have destroyed her early memorabilia. See M. Hazzard, *Australia's Brilliant Daughter, Ellis Rowan: Artist, Naturalist, Explorer, 1848–1922* (Melbourne: Greenhouse Publications, 1984), p. 22.

3 Before arriving in Australia, John Cotton had published two books on English birds and had intended to write and illustrate another on the birds of the Port Phillip District before he died in 1849, aged 47. It was subsequently published by M. Casey, *John Cotton's Birds of the Port Phillip District of New South Wales 1843–1849* (Melbourne: William Collins, 1974).

4 Ellis Rowan was not the only member of the family to devote her life to depicting and preserving nature: her brother Charles became a famous doctor and hero of the 1870s Turkish wars, and later a founding member of the Royal Australian Ornithologists Union; and her cousins, the Le Souefs, established the first zoos in Melbourne, Sydney and Perth. Her aunt, Caroline (née Cotton), painted decorative boxes containing miniature Aboriginal weapons carved by her husband Albert Le Souef.

5 Ellis Agar Hartley was Charles Ryan's mother. See M. Clarke, *Clarke of Rupertswood (1831–1897)* (Melbourne: Australian Scholarly Publishing, 1995), p. 58, quoting Burke's Colonial Gentry.

6 M. Hazzard and H. Hewson, *Flower Paintings of Ellis Rowan from the Collection of the National Library of Australia*. Canberra: National Library of Australia, 1982, p. 1.

7 A. Colquhuon, 'Australian Artists of the Past: Mrs Ellis Rowan', *Age*, 4 March 1933.

8 Hazzard, op. cit., p. 24 (quoting 'Rare Flowers on Canvas: She Never Took Lessons', *New York Times*, 16 January 1898).

9 Ibid., p. 33. *Derriweit Heights* was razed to the ground in the bush-fires of 1983.

10 It was von Mueller's great disappointment that he had to hand over his botanical work to Sir Joseph Hooker, Director of the Royal Botanic Gardens in Kew, for a collaboration with George Bentham, resulting in the publication of *Flora Australiensis (1863–1878)* in seven volumes. See H. Hewson, *Australia: 300 years of Botanical Illustration* (Melbourne: CSIRO Publishing, 1999), p. 130.

11 E. Rowan, 'Making an Art Collection', in *The Oarswoman*, Brisbane, December 1912.

12 *New York Times*, 16 January, 1898.

13 Rowan, op. cit., 1991, Preface.

14 A. Garran (ed.), *Australia: The First Hundred Years*. 3 Vols. Sydney: The Picturesque Atlas Publishing Company Ltd., 1886; reprinted Sydney: Paul Hamlyn, 1978.

15 Rowan's four-leaved screen 'was the most prominent feature of attraction. It consists of beautiful arrangements of native flowers of Victoria, New Zealand and New South Wales, executed in water colours upon black, pale yellow, pale blue and crimson satin.' *Official Record, Melbourne International Exhibition 1880–1881*. Melbourne: Commissioners, Mason, Firth and McCutcheon, 1882, p. 427; Hazzard, op. cit., p. 38.

16 *The Temple of Flora* was published by Robert Thornton between 1799 and 1807. See Wilfred Blunt and William T. Stearn, *The Art of Botanical Illustration*. London: Antique Collector's Club, 1995, p. 236–243.

17 Ellis Rowan, 'An Australian Artist's Adventures', *New Idea*, 6 February 1905, p. 714.

18 H. Vellacott (ed.), *Some Recollections of a Happy Life: Marianne North in Australia and New Zealand*. Melbourne: Edward Arnold Australia, 1986, p. 66.

19 *The Calcutta Englishman*, Calcutta, 27 November 1893.

20 *Australasia Illustrated* was the brainchild of the Hon. Andrew Garran, journalist and politician. Similar to contemporary American publications at the time, it was designed to give an illustrated and summarised Australasian history up to the 1880s,

covering each colony with its exploration and development, it was filled with over 700 illustrations. For comments on the publication see A. Sayers, *Drawing in Australia: Watercolours, Pastels and Collages 1770s to 1980s*. Melbourne: Oxford University Press and National Gallery of Australia, 1998, p. 116.

21 *Official Record of the Centennial International Exhibition, Melbourne, 1888–1889*. Melbourne: Sands and McDougall, 1890. *Chrysanthemums* fetched a record price of $88,000 at a Christies' auction, Melbourne, in 1989.

22 *Argus*, Melbourne, 25 January 1889; Hazzard, op. cit., p. 51.

23 Tom Roberts refused to acknowledge her presence when they met on Murray Island, north of Cape York, in 1892. See Rowan, op. cit., 1991, p. 130 and McKay, *Ellis Rowan: A Flower-Hunter in Queensland* (Brisbane: Queensland Museum, 1990), p. 24–26. As late as 1935, Roberts' friend Arthur Streeton wrote that his painting *Spring Pastoral*, had been restored by 'amateur hands (Mrs Ellis Rowan)' (*The Arthur Streeton Catalogue*. Melbourne: Arthur Streeton, 1935, p. 114). Now in the collection of the National Gallery of Victoria, this painting is about to be displayed as a key work in the forthcoming opening of Federation Square in Melbourne.

24 The 12 panels at The Australian Club are of various subjects ranging from waterlilies to tropical palms, painted on butcher's paper and attached to the walls by an embossed gold border. No photographs are known of her wall decoration at *Cliveden*, but a photograph of one of her screens *in situ* is reproduced in A. Montana, *The Art Movement in Australia: Design, Taste and Society 1875–1900* (Melbourne, Miegunyah Press, 2000), p. 153. A photograph of her murals at the Victorian Racing Club Dining Room can be seen at the Australian Racing Museum, Caulfield (VRM11795).

25 J. Gooding, *Margaret Forrest, Wildflowers of Western Australia*. Perth: Art Gallery of Western Australia, 1984, p. 10; Hazzard, op. cit., p. 112.

26 J. McKay, op. cit., p. 9–12.

27 Rowan, op. cit., 1991, p. 12.

28 Ibid., p. 29.

29 Ibid., p. 95. In her writing Rowan never let the facts get in the way of a good story, a point she passed on to her nieces, Maie Casey and Joice Nankivell Loch, who both became internationally recognised and wrote books in a style inspired by their aunt. Sir Rex de Charembac Nan Kivell (1898–1977), a major donor to the collections of the National Library of Australia, was a self-made parvenu of New Zealand origins, who, according to Maie Casey, was a distant relation to the family. See John Ritchie (ed.), *Australian Dictionary of Biography*. Vol. 15 (1940–1980). Melbourne: Melbourne University Press, 2000, p. 460.

30 The economic depression of the early 1890s caused bankruptcy and ruin for many Melbourne businessmen, including Rowan's family. As much as her father Charles Ryan fought the prospect of bankruptcy, in 1896 he was eventually forced to sell his beloved *Derriweit Heights*, moving his remaining family into the small gardener's cottage on the property.

31 In the same competition Tom Roberts and A.H. Fullwood won awards for oils; Lister Lister, Fullwood and Ellis Rowan for watercolours.

32 Letter to Ellis Rowan from Windsor Castle, 17 May 1895. In her cuttings book Rowan pasted the telegram from Windsor Castle on the opening page (Manuscripts Collection, National Library of Australia (MS2206)).

33 Rowan later claimed that Lord Leighton said her collection was unique and valued it at £15,000 (see *Queenslander*, 10 June 1911). See also J. McKay, 'Ellis Rowan, a Flower Hunter', *Art in Australia*, vol. 27, Winter 1990, p. 579. Leighton's praise was later included in the publicity generated for Rowan's 1920 travelling exhibition to America, (see Manuscript Collection, National Library of Australia (MS806)). See also Hazzard, op. cit., p. 112.

34 *Sketch*, London, 20 May 1896. For the first time Rowan's work was compared with her mentor, Marianne North, raising the issue as to whether it was art or botany: 'To botanists and horticulturists the series should be very interesting just as Miss Marianne North's drawings at the Museum in the Kew Gardens … but neither in one case or the other are the drawings to be considered art.' (Hazzard, op. cit., p. 89, quoting *The Bazaar*).

35 *The British Australian*, 4 January 1896. For further reviews see Hazzard, op. cit., p. 88–90.

36 Ibid., p. 90.

37 A new colour printing process is described in the preface to Alice Lounsberry, *A Guide to the Wild Flowers* (New York: Frederick A. Stokes and Co., 1899), with its 64 coloured and 100 black and white plates. Rowan had 12 paintings from that publication made into a portfolio for sale at US$5.00. In 1980 one of these folios sold in Melbourne for $1200 (see Hazzard, op. cit. p. 98).

38 Hazzard, op. cit., p. 97.

39 Ibid., p. 104.

40 Bill Baillie became her constant friend and travelling companion for several years and she wrote of their times together in an enchanting children's book *Bill Baillie: His Life and Adventures*, written in Adelaide and published in 1908 (Melbourne: Whitcombe and Tombs) with pen sketches by John Sommers. The dedication read: 'to Miss Winifred Scott of Adelaide without whose sympathetic help and advice the story … would probably never have been written'. It was reprinted in 1948 as *Bill Baillie: The Story of a Pet Bilboa* (ibid.).

41 Hazzard, op. cit., p. 106.

42 At the Society Art Rooms, North Terrace.

43 'As London has its North Gallery, why should not Melbourne have its Rowan Gallery?', *Age*, 8 December 1909.

44 H.A. Tardent, *Mrs Ellis Rowan and her Contributions to Australian Art and Science*. Brisbane: Watson, Ferguson and Co., 1927, p. 20.

45 'The Romance of Flowers: The Beauty of New Guinea', *Herald*, 1 December 1916.

46 In April 2002, one of the large Titan Arums flowered at the Royal Botanic Gardens in Kew, attracting large crowds and much publicity. See www.kew.org/titan/images.html

47 *Herald*, 1 December 1916, op. cit..

48 'Painting Rare Birds', *Argus*, Melbourne, 9 November 1918.

49 Letters, Ellis Rowan to Sir Baldwin Spencer, 7 and 10 January 1918, Museum Victoria Archives.

50 *Sun*, 13 March 1918. The fungi are reproduced in C. Barrett, *Australian Wildlife* (Melbourne: Georgian House, 1945).

51 *Argus*, Melbourne, 23 January 1919.

52 George Meudell (1860–1936) wrote a controversial book exposing some of the nefarious dealings of the Melbourne land boom. See M. Cannon, *The Land Boomers*. Melbourne: Melbourne University Press, 1966, chapter 9, 'The Meudell Mystery'.

53 *Brooklyn Eagle*, 3 August 1919; *New York Times*, 24 August 1919.

54 Most of the American works remained in Maie Casey's collection. Some were presented to various institutions and the rest remained in the hands of her family. Some were sold at Josef Lebovic Gallery, Sydney, on 24 May 1990, and at the Australian Galleries, Melbourne, in May 1999.

55 H. Sandon, *Royal Worcester Porcelain from 1862 to the Present Day*. London: Barrie and Jenkins, 1973.

56 Judith McKay suggests that Rowan visited Kuranda in 1911 and probably first saw the Dodd collection at that time; see McKay, op. cit., p. 27. For an account of the Dodd collection, see Geoff Monteith, *The Butterfly Man from Kuranda, Frederick Parkhurst Dodd* (Brisbane: Queensland Museum, 1991).

57 For many years they remained in her sister's, Ada Scott's English residence, *Boughton House*, but when 36 sheets sold at Christies' in London in 1995, they fetched a record price of £183,900. See *Christies' London Auction Catalogue* (London: Christies, Manson and Woods), 16 May 1995, Lots 201–222, 'Watercolours and Pictures of Birds and Ellis Rowan's Butterflies and Moths of New Guinea', sold in aid of the Merlin Trust, with 'An Origin of the Material Illustrated' written by R.J. Vane-Wright, Department of Entomology at the Natural History Museum.

58 Hazzard, op. cit., p. 130. The letter was dated 17 June, but without mention of the year nor the recipient. It was probably written in 1918 or 1919, as the butterflies were exhibited in Rowan's grand show at Anthony Hordern's in March 1920.

59 Ibid., p. 133.

60 William Moore, *The Story of Australian Art*. Vol. 2. Sydney: Angus and Robertson, 1934, p. 33.

61 Hazzard, op. cit., p. 131.

62 House of Representatives, *Hansard*, 24 August 1923.

63 'Mrs Rowan's Pictures: To Buy or Not to Buy, "Disastrous Art", Opinions of Leading Artists', *Sun*, Sydney, 17 January 1923.

64 *White Paper: Proposed Purchase of Mrs Ellis Rowan's Collection of Drawings*, presented in the House of Representatives, 1 December 1921.

65 Winifred Scott, 'An Appreciation', *Ellis Rowan's newspaper cuttings book 1895–1922*, Manuscript Collection, National Library of Australia (MS2203).

BIOGRAPHY

1848

Marian Ellis Ryan born 30 July in Melbourne; the eldest of Charles Ryan and Marian Cotton's seven children; known as Ellis from an early age.

1849

John Cotton, her maternal grandfather, dies aged 47; leaves sketchbooks to Ellis Rowan. Charles Ryan leases *Killeen Station*, Longwood.

1854

Ryan family move to Brighton; father sets up Ryan and Hammond, Estate Agents and Cattle Auctioneers, Melbourne. Ellis attends Miss Murphy's school in Brighton.

1860

Mother, Marian Ryan, returns to England. Ellis goes to boarding school at *Earimil* on the Mornington Peninsula.

1861

Mother returns to Australia and the Ryan family move to *Vaucluse* in Richmond.

1869

Her future husband, Frederic Rowan, injured in New Zealand Maori Wars; visits Melbourne on way to the United Kingdom, April to December; probably meets Charles Ryan at Melbourne Club.

1869–1870

Visits England; probably takes painting lessons.

1871

Frederic Rowan returns to New Zealand in January as Sub-Inspector for Constabulary of Armed Forces.

1872

Wins bronze medal for four panels of Australian wildflowers at Intercolonial Exhibition Melbourne. Father buys 26 acres on Mount Macedon and starts the historic garden at *Derriweit Heights*.

1873

Engaged to Captain Frederic Charles Rowan in June; married 23 October. The Rowans go to Pukearuhe, North Island, New Zealand, in December; under her husband's guidance she paints native flora.

1875

Returns pregnant to *Derriweit Heights* in January; paints panels and screens. Frederic Charles Eric Elliott Rowan, known as Puck, born 13 July. Returns to New Zealand.

1877

Rowans move to Melbourne, Punt Road, Richmond; Frederic Rowan becomes manager of Electric Light Power and Storage Company, representative of Pacific Telegraph Company, Vice-President of Victorian Engineers Association and a member of the board of Melbourne Tram and Omnibus Company. Travels Australia with her husband.

1879

Wins silver medal at International and Intercolonial Exhibition, Sydney.

1880

Opening of Exhibition Buildings Melbourne in October; wins gold medal for four-leaved screen on satin, plus special merit for ten framed groups of wildflowers on satin. Meets Marianne North in Albany, Western Australia, who probably instructs her in oil painting. North goes to Tasmania with Ferdinand von Mueller and visits Ryans at *Derriweit Heights*.

1883

Travels with sister Blanche to visit her sister Ada (Lady Scott) in England via India, Ceylon and Europe in March; in Calcutta wins gold medal; Amsterdam, silver medal; St Petersburg, gold medal.

1884

Frederic Rowan's father dies in Copenhagen; Frederic appointed Consul for Denmark. Ellis wins prize for lace-making in Denmark.

1887

Goes to Queensland during winter; does some of her best work, over 100 engravings of flowers and scenes published in *Australasia Illustrated* (other artists include Tom Roberts, Conrad Martens, Henry Fullwood and Louis Buvelot, but most executed by George and Julian Ashton and Ellis Rowan).

1888

International Exhibition, Melbourne Exhibition Building; wins First Order of Merit and Gold Medal for *Chrysanthemums*, second prize for *Marguerites*; Adelaide Jubilee Exhibition; wins five first awards and gold medal.

1889

Visits Western Australia, September to October; painting tour with Margaret Forrest to Boolantha Station, north of Carnarvon and Geraldton; sketches spring flowers. Exhibits at Railway Station Reading Room in Perth in November. Son Puck, expelled from Melbourne Grammar School aged 14, after Melbourne Cup prank.

1891

Exhibition at Buxton's Art Gallery, Swanston Street, Melbourne, October.

1892

Second trip to Queensland with Puck in winter; visits Normanby, Rockhampton, Mount Morgan, Mackay, Thursday Island, Cape York, Cooktown, Somerset, Murray Island (meets Tom Roberts), Jervis Island, Cairns, Hambledon, Muldiva, Chillagoe Caves, Barron Falls, Myola and Herberton. Sixty-five flower paintings sent to von Mueller for identification. Letters to Frederic Rowan from this trip form the first part of her autobiography. Husband, Frederic Rowan, dies of what was thought to be pneumonia aged 47 on 6 December. Ellis goes to live at *Derriweit Heights*.

1893

Exhibits 99 paintings in World Columbian Exhibition, Chicago, her last international competition; wins gold medal (Tom Roberts, A.H. Fullwood awards for oils; Lister Lister, Fullwood and Rowan for watercolours). To date total of 29 medals (ten gold, 15 silver and four bronze); holds solo shows from now on with works that can be sold. Visits New Zealand; letters to family form latter half of her autobiography; paints black and white landscapes reproduced in *The Town and Country Journal* in December.

1894

Returns to Melbourne.

1895

Takes paintings to London in April where brother Cecil Ryan is Lieutenant Commander of the Victorian Horse Artillery; stays with sister Ada Scott in Knightsbridge; visits Windsor Castle in May, meets Queen Victoria who chooses three paintings for a screen.

1896

Exhibits 100 paintings of Australian wildflowers at Dowdeswell Galleries, New Bond Street, Mayfair, in April; exhibition opened by Duchess of Teck who buys three works; many favourable reviews, including one by Lord Leighton. Receives commissions for murals and oil paintings. Meets German Chancellor Prince von Bismarck whom she claims offers her the position of government botanist for Germany, and to purchase her collection for £15,000. *Derriweit Heights* sold; Ryan family move into gardener's cottage.

1897

Writes preface for her autobiography in London in November. Puck dies 5 December, aged 22 in a Mashonaland Gaol. Goes to New York; meets Dr N.L. Britton, Director of New York Botanical Gardens, and botanist Alice Lounsberry.

1898

Publishes autobiography *A Flower-Hunter in Queensland and New Zealand* (London: John Murray). Learns of Puck's death. Father Charles Ryan dies.

1899

Illustrates *A Guide to the Wildflowers* by Alice Lounsberry (New York: Frederick A. Stokes Co.); contributes 64 coloured and 100 black and white plates. Twelve colour plates reproduced in separate portfolios priced at US$5.00 each.

1900

Illustrates *A Guide to the Trees* by Alice Lounsberry (New York: Frederick A. Stokes Co.); contributes 64 coloured and 164 black and white plates. Undergoes cosmetic face-lift; reduces her said-age by ten years.

1901

Illustrates *Southern Wildflowers and Trees* by Alice Lounsberry (New York: Frederick A. Stokes Co.); contributes 16 coloured and 161 black and white plates. Exhibits at Field Columbian Museum, Chicago in May. Visits Florida, Cuba and the Caribbean; returns to New York in December.

1902

Exhibits at Clausen's Gallery, 381 Fifth Ave, New York, January to February, 500 paintings of wildflowers of the United States, West Indies, Australia and New Zealand.

1904

Travels the United States to Mexican border, across the Sierras to California, to Stanford University and Panama-Pacific Exposition. Probably returns to Melbourne. Exhibits at Scourfield Chambers, 163 Collins Street, Melbourne, in December.

1905

Starts landscape classes with John Mather in Melbourne.

1906

Visits Western Australia: Kalgoorlie, Laverton and Goongarrie. Given pet bilby, Bill Baillie. Exhibits at Australian Natives' Association Hall, Hannan Street, Kalgoorlie.

1907

Exhibits in *Australian Exhibition of Women's Work*, 66 Hay Street, Perth. Goes to Adelaide, Broken Hill; exhibition at Society Art Rooms, North Terrace, Adelaide. South Australian Government buys 100 works for £1000. Sir John Downer buys 20, which are bequeathed to the South Australian Government by his brother George.

1908

Publishes *Bill Baillie: His Life and Adventures* (Melbourne:

Whitcombe and Tombs) with eight watercolour landscapes by Rowan, sketches by John Sommers. Returns to Melbourne; travels by train to paint in Gippsland and the Grampians, Victoria.

1909

Exhibits at Scourfields Chambers, 163 Collins Street, Melbourne, in December.

1910

Exhibits at Bernard's Gallery, Collins Street, Melbourne, 5–31 July. Exhibits at Angus and Robertson Gallery, Sydney, 25 July – 13 August. Sydney Technical College buys 65 paintings.

1911

Visits Queensland in June: Brisbane, Rockhampton, Longreach, Townsville, Cardwell, Dungeness, Dunk Island and Kuranda, where she probably sees the Dodd butterfly collection. Stays with her cousins the Nankivells on Herbert River; paints spotted orchid named in her honour; agitates for her collection to be bought by Queensland Government; returns to Melbourne.

1912

Returns to Queensland. Exhibits at Old Town Hall, Queen Street, Brisbane, 5 August – 14 September. Queensland Government buys 100 paintings for £1000; gives them an extra 25 for £50. Returns to Melbourne.

1913

Returns to Queensland, June to September; contributes 16 colour plates to publication of *A Comprehensive Catalogue of Queensland Plants* by Frederick Bailley (Brisbane: A.J. Cumming Government Printer).

1914

Mother Marian Ryan dies. Sells paintings for £25 each, raising £6000 for war cause. Practises the art of china painting for Sydney jeweller and importer of fine china, Flavelle Brothers, who send her designs to Royal Worcester Porcelain Company, England. Exhibits at Fine Art Society's Rooms, Collins Street, Melbourne, in December; 95 paintings selling from £1.50 to £105 each.

1915

Exhibits at Anthony Hordern's Gallery, New Palace Emporium, Brickfield Hill, Sydney, 25 March to mid April.

1916

Travels to Papua New Guinea, now an Australian protectorate after German occupancy for many years, in May, aged 68. Exhibits at Technical College, Harris Street, Sydney, in November; bird of paradise paintings for sale as a collection only; flowers on circular

maroon-bordered paper intended for dessert plates by Flavelle Brothers for Royal Worcester Porcelain Company, bought by Kew Gardens Herbarium in London.

1917

Returns to New Guinea to paint the birds of paradise in April; exhibition in German store, Madang Mission House; paints 25 birds (19 caught live), fungi and flowers in the Bismarck Ranges; contracts malaria. Returns to Macedon Cottage; nursed by sister Blanche Ryan.

1918

Writes to Sir Baldwin Spencer requesting access to paint the stuffed birds at the Melbourne Museum. Exhibits at Fine Art Society's Galleries, Alfred Place, Melbourne, 6–19 November; 40 birds of paradise, 72 fungi, 172 flowers, two coral, a bat, a squirrel and a fish.

1919

Touring exhibition at Stanford University, California, via other venues to American Museum of Natural History, New York. Paints 2175 butterflies and moths at *Widgiewa*, New South Wales, during winter. Paints birds of paradise for Flavelle Brothers.

1920

Exhibits at Anthony Hordern's Gallery, New Palace Emporium, Brickfield Hill, Sydney, 2–31 March; 1000 paintings, largest ever solo exhibition held to date in Australia, all works for sale except the birds of paradise; £2000 sold, making a record for a woman artist. Stays at *Widgiewa* in the Riverina during winter. Writes letters to Prime Minister William Hughes regarding the future of her collection.

1921

Stays at *Widgiewa* during winter. Requests £20,000 for her collection, or £6000 and a copra plantation in New Guinea instead. Debate in Parliament over purchase of the Ellis Rowan Collection by the Commonwealth Government in November.

1922

Dies 4 October at Macedon; buried in family grave at Mount Macedon.

1923

£5000 paid to sister Blanche Ryan, sole survivor and executrix of the Rowan estate, for purchase of 947 watercolours of Australian and New Guinean subjects.

1927

Henry Tardent publishes *Mrs Ellis Rowan and her Contributions to Australian Art and Science* (Brisbane: Watson, Ferguson and Co.).

1962

First solo exhibition of her works since her death, South Australian

Museum, North Terrace, Adelaide. Helen Jo Samuel publishes *Wild Flower Hunter: The Story of Ellis Rowan*, with illustrations by Maie Casey, London.

1963

Maie Casey organises an exhibition of works from her own collection at Qantas Gallery, Piccadilly, London in June.

1966

The Lindsay Report suggests that the Ellis Rowan Collection, along with works from the Nan Kivell and Hardy Wilson Collections be housed at the proposed National Gallery of Australia.

1982

In March, solo exhibition of 20 paintings at the National Library of Australia, in conjunction with publication of *Flower Paintings of Ellis Rowan from the Collection of the National Library of Australia* by Margaret Hazzard and Helen Hewson.

1988

Exhibition *A Festival of Ellis Rowan Flower Paintings*, at *Yarrabee*, Botanic Gardens of Adelaide, South Australia, 26 February to 26 March, 1988 (49 watercolours, 21 pieces of porcelain and a screen).

1989

Chrysanthemums fetches a record price of $88,000 at Christies' Auction, Melbourne, in May.

1990

Exhibition, *Ellis Rowan: A Flower-Hunter in Queensland*, Queensland Museum, Brisbane, in conjunction with a publication of the same name by Judith McKay. Tours to Queensland Regional Galleries and to Sydney, Hobart and Christchurch, New Zealand, 1990 to 1997.

1995

Thirty-six sheets of butterflies sell at Christies' Auction in London, 16 May, and fetch a record price of £183,900.

Mrs Rowan in the Heart of Papua
published in *Woman's World*, 1 December 1922

[*Christmas Bells (Blandfordia), Flax Lily (Dianella), Haemodorum and Grasses*]
1879
Western Australia
gouache and watercolour on paper; 53.7 x 37.2 cm
nla.pic–an6724147 Pictures Collection R2069

**[*Geebung (Persoonia), Showy Dryandra (Dryandra formosa),*
(Chorizema diversifolium)]** 1880
Albany, Western Australia
gouache and watercolour on paper; 54.4 x 37.9 cm
nla.pic–an6766312 Pictures Collection R2310

[*Rose Cone Flower (Isopogon formosus), Conesticks (Petrophile diversifolia and Petrophile serruriae),*
Pixie Mops (Petrophile macrostachya), Cone Bush (Isopogon teretifolia)] 1880
Western Australia
gouache and watercolour on paper; 54.5 x 38.0 cm
nla.pic–an6766367 Pictures Collection R2457

[Trigger Plant (Stylidium), Morning Flag (Orthrosanthus multiflorus), Fan Flower (Scaevola porocarya),

Stackhousia, Chamaescilla, Dampiera] 1880

Champion Bay, Western Australia

gouache and watercolour on paper; 54.5 x 38.0 cm

nla.pic–an6765433 Pictures Collection R2384

[*Black Kangaroo Paw (Macropidia fuliginosa), Red and Green or Mangles' Kangaroo Paw
(Anigozanthos manglesii), Cats Paw (Anigozanthos humilis)*] c.1880
Perth, Western Australia
gouache and watercolour on paper; 54.7 x 38.0 cm
nla.pic–an6632773 Pictures Collection R2028

[*(Abutilon), Emu Bush (Eremophila)*] c.1880

Carnarvon, Western Australia

gouache and watercolour on paper; 54.7 x 37.8 cm

nla.pic–an6764648 Pictures Collection R2382

Albizzia vaillantii 1887

Johnstone River, Queensland

gouache and watercolour on paper; 54.8 x 38.0 cm

nla.pic–an6730561 Pictures Collection R2142

[*Berries and Fruit*] 1887
Johnstone River, Queensland
gouache and watercolour on paper; 54.7 x 38.0 cm
nla.pic–an6766409 Pictures Collection R2625

Crinum longiflora 1887
Queensland
gouache and watercolour on paper; 54.7 x 37.9 cm
nla.pic–an6723088 Pictures Collection R2626

Harpullia hillii [*Tulipwood*], ***Mackinlaya macrosciadia*** 1887
Mackay, Queensland
gouache and watercolour on paper; 54.6 x 38.0 cm
nla.pic–an6723385 Pictures Collection R2569

Mucuna gigantea [*Velvet Bean*], *Nepenthes phyllamphora* [*Pitcher Plant*],
Geitonoplesium cymosum [*Scrambling Lily*] 1887
Mackay, Queensland
gouache and watercolour on paper; 54.5 x 38.0 cm
nla.pic–an6722787 Pictures Collection R2643

Pandanus pedunculatus [***Beach Pandan***] 1887
Mackay, Queensland
gouache and watercolour on paper; 54.5 x 38.0 cm
nla.pic–an6649839 Pictures Collection R2109

[*Rock Lily (Dendrobium speciosum)*] 1887
Queensland
gouache and watercolour on paper; 54.7 x 38.0 cm
nla.pic–an6723370 Pictures Collection R2576

Tylophora grandiflora, Hemigenia purpurea, Eremophila bignoniflora [*Bignonia Emu Bush*] 1887
Queensland
gouache and watercolour on paper; 54.7 x 38.8 cm
nla.pic–an6723118 Pictures Collection R2608

[*Cockatoo or Cocky Apple (Planchonia careya), Morning Glory (Ipomoea sinuata)*] c.1887
Dungeness, Herbert River, Queensland
gouache and watercolour on paper; 54.8 x 38.0 cm
nla.pic–an6649745 Pictures Collection R2102

Coleus scuttelarioides, Murdannia graminea, Aneilema gramineum, Commelinaceae c.1887

Queensland

gouache and watercolour on paper; 54.0 x 37.5 cm

nla.pic–an6649803 Pictures Collection R2092

Costus, Artanema fimbriatum, Tabernaemontana pubescens c.1887

Herbert River, Queensland

gouache and watercolour on paper; 54.7 x 38.0 cm

nla.pic–an6732441 Pictures Collection R2239

Crinum sp. [***Lily***] c.1887

Queensland

gouache and watercolour on paper; 56.0 x 38.0 cm

nla.pic–an6649819 Pictures Collection R2096

[*Dendrobium discolor*] c.1887
Queensland
gouache and watercolour on paper; 54.5 x 38.0 cm
nla.pic–an6732402 Pictures Collection R2218

***Melastoma malabathricum* [*Pink Lasiandra*], *Wormia alata*, *Lygodium scandens* [*Maidenhair Fern*]** c.1887
Herbert River, Queensland
gouache and watercolour on paper; 54.8 x 38.2 cm
nla.pic–an6731136 Pictures Collection R2180

Phaius tankervilliae, Dendrobium cacatua, Dendrobium delicatum c.1887

'Obtained at Brisbane painted in Mackay', Queensland

gouache and watercolour on paper; 54.7 x 38.0 cm

nla.pic–an6732414 Pictures Collection R2224

[*Gymea Lily (Doryanthes excelsa)*] c.1887–1889
New South Wales (?)
gouache and watercolour on paper; 76.2 x 55.0 cm
nla.pic–an7677462 Pictures Collection R2547

***Grevillea leucopteris* [*Plume Grevillea*]** c.1889

Western Australia

gouache and watercolour on paper; 53.3 x 35.5 cm

nla.pic–an7719035 Pictures Collection R2436

Halgania corymbosa, Spinifex longifolius, Stylobasium spatulatum c.1889
Carnarvon, Western Australia
gouache and watercolour on paper; 54.0 x 37.3 cm
nla.pic–an6730522 Pictures Collection R2131

Lilac Hibiscus (Alyogyne huegelii) c.1889

Champion Bay, Western Australia

gouache and watercolour on paper; 54.7 x 38.0 cm

nla.pic–an6735435 Pictures Collection R2353

[*Native Hibiscus, Unidentified Flowers and Berries*] c.1889
Western Australia
gouache and watercolour on paper; 54.5 x 38.0 cm
nla.pic–an6766405 Pictures Collection R2616

[*Sturt's Desert Pea (Swainsona formosa)*] c.1889
Western Australia (?)
gouache and watercolour on paper; 54.5 x 38.0 cm
nla.pic–an23309851 Pictures Collection R2589

Dendrobium atroviolaceum [*Tree Orchid and Forest*] c.1890–1892
Queensland
gouache and watercolour on paper; 55.7 x 38.0 cm
nla.pic–an23620871 Pictures Collection R1805

Albizzia lucyi c.1892

Gertrude River, Queensland

gouache and watercolour on paper; 54.8 x 38.2 cm

nla.pic–an6649824 Pictures Collection R2100

[*Golden Bouquet Tree (Deplanchea tetraphylla)*] c.1892
Somerset, Queensland
gouache and watercolour on paper; 54.5 x 38.0 cm
nla.pic–an6820611 Pictures Collection R2379

[*Gymea Lily (Doryanthes excelsa*)] c.1892
New South Wales (?)
gouache and watercolour on paper; 76.0 x 56.2 cm
nla.pic–an7677432 Pictures Collection R2540

Hibiscus heterophyllus [*Native Rosella*] c.1892
New South Wales
gouache and watercolour on paper; 55.0 x 38.0 cm
nla.pic–an6724343 Pictures Collection R2179

[*Old Man or Saw Banksia (Banksia serrata)*] c.1892
Queensland
gouache and watercolour on paper; 76.0 x 56.2 cm
nla.pic–an7677454 Pictures Collection R2543

[*Screw Pine (Pandanus)*] c.1892
Johnstone River, Queensland
gouache and watercolour on paper; 54.5 x 38.0 cm
nla.pic–an6731160 Pictures Collection R2200

Solanum aculeatissimum c.1892
Inscribed on reverse 'A South American plant, a naturalised weed in Queensland'
gouache and watercolour on paper; 56.0 x 37.6 cm
nla.pic—an6723081 Pictures Collection R2638

***Metrosideros sp.* [*New Zealand Christmas Bush*]** c.1893
New Zealand
gouache and watercolour on paper; 56.2 x 76.0 cm
nla.pic–an23621177 Pictures Collection R2552

[*Sugar Gum (Eucalyptus cladocalyx)*] c.1906
South Australia
gouache and watercolour on paper; 73.4 x 54.0 cm
nla.pic–an7677426 Pictures Collection R2536

***Bombax malabaricum* [*Red Silk Cotton Tree*]** c.1911
Queensland
gouache and watercolour on paper; 56.0 x 38.2 cm
nla.pic–an6731148 Pictures Collection R2190

*Castanospermum australe [**Black Bean or Moreton Bay Chestnut**]* c.1911

Queensland

gouache and watercolour on paper; 56.0 x 38.0 cm

nla.pic–an6732490 Pictures Collection R2242

Eugenia cormiflora c.1911

Barron River, Queensland

gouache and watercolour on paper; 56.0 x 38.0 cm

nla.pic–an6730510 Pictures Collection R2130

Large Tree Orchid with Papilio sp. [*Citrus Butterflies*] c.1911

Queensland

gouache and watercolour on paper; 76.2 x 56.0 cm

nla.pic—an23620971 Pictures Collection R1790

Phaleria macrocarpa c.1911

Queensland

gouache and watercolour on paper; 56.1 x 36.2 cm

nla.pic–an23620968 Pictures Collection R2377

[*Cockatoo or Cocky Apple (Planchonia careya)*] c.1911–1913
Dungeness, Herbert River, Queensland
gouache and watercolour on paper; 55.0 x 38.5 cm
nla.pic–an6729949 Pictures Collection R2474

Coral Tree (Erythrina lysistemon) c.1911–1913
Queensland
gouache and watercolour on paper; 54.7 x 38.0 cm
nla.pic–an6724415 Pictures Collection R2165

Delarbrea michieana c.1911–1913
Queensland
gouache and watercolour on paper; 56.0 x 38.0 cm
nla.pic–an6731151 Pictures Collection R2192

Pimelea haematostachya [*Flinders Poppy*] c.1911–1913
Queensland
gouache and watercolour on paper; 56.0 x 38.0 cm
nla.pic–an6724418 Pictures Collection R2162

Syzygium sp. c.1911–1913

Queensland

gouache and watercolour on paper; 75.0 x 56.3 cm

nla.pic–an23621312 Pictures Collection R2538

Acalypha sp. with Troides oblongomaculatus [*Birdwing Butterfly*] c.1916–1917

Papua New Guinea

gouache and watercolour on paper; 76.0 x 55.9 cm

nla.pic–an23621280 Pictures Collection R1757

***Amaranthus caudatus* [*Tassel Flower*]** c.1916–1917
Papua New Guinea
gouache and watercolour on paper; 78.5 x 60.2 cm
nla.pic–an23621303 Pictures Collection R1922

[*Pendulous Orange Seed Pods*] c.1916–1917

Papua New Guinea

gouache and watercolour on paper; 75.8 x 56.0 cm

nla.pic–an23621128 Pictures Collection R1770

Family Araliaceae with Parthenos sylvia [**The Clipper**] c.1916–1917
Papua New Guinea
gouache and watercolour on paper; 76.1 x 55.8 cm
nla.pic–an23621147 Pictures Collection R1759

Lamiodendron magnificum c.1916–1917

Papua New Guinea

gouache and watercolour on paper; 75.9 x 55.9 cm

nla.pic–an23621201 Pictures Collection R1730

[*Leaves and Flowers of Plant from Papua New Guinea*] c.1916–1917
Papua New Guinea
gouache and watercolour on paper; 76.0 x 56.0 cm
nla.pic–an5597941 Pictures Collection R1791

Rubiaceae c.1916–1917

Papua New Guinea

gouache and watercolour on paper; 76.2 x 56.0 cm

nla.pic–an23621261 Pictures Collection R1779

[*Amorphophallus Flower and Fruit*] c.1916–1917
Papua New Guinea
gouache and watercolour on paper; 78.3 x 58.7 cm
nla.pic–an6647795 Pictures Collection R1729

[*Netted Stinkhorn Fungus, Dictyophora phalloidea or Dictyophora multicolor*] c.1916–1917

Papua New Guinea

gouache and watercolour on paper; 28.0 x 19.0 cm

From the collection of Anna Macgowan

Count Raggi's Bird of Paradise (Paradisaea raggiana) c.1917
Papua New Guinea
gouache and watercolour on paper; 76.0 x 56.0 cm
nla.pic–an6633332 Pictures Collection R1963

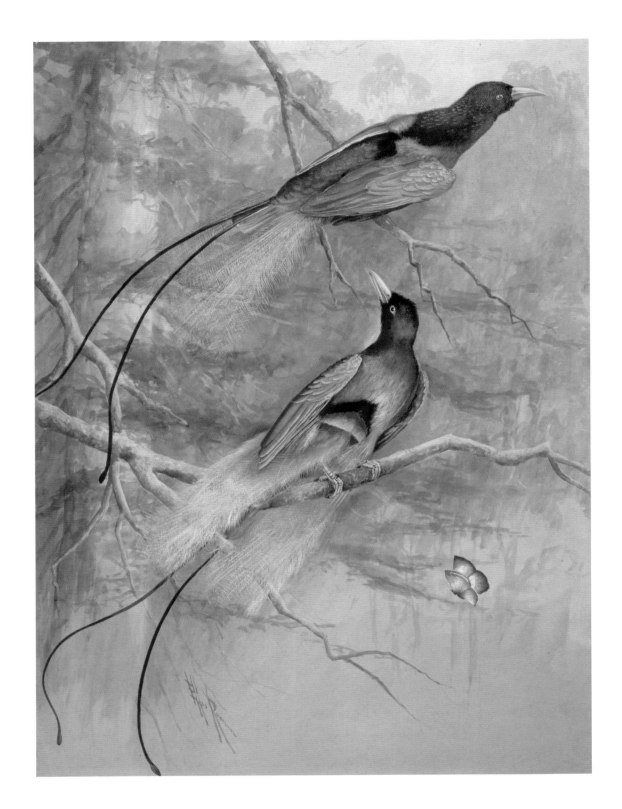

[*Elliot's Bird of Paradise*] c.1917
Papua New Guinea
gouache and watercolour on paper; 76.1 x 55.5 cm
nla.pic–an6633334 Pictures Collection R1962

Rothschild's Bird of Paradise (Astrapia rothschildi) c.1917
Papua New Guinea
gouache and watercolour on paper; 76.5 x 56.2 cm
nla.pic–an6633368 Pictures Collection R1949

[*Goldie's Bird of Paradise (Paradisaea decora)*] c.1917
gouache and watercolour on muslin; 16.5 cm diameter
nla.pic–an23715478 Pictures Collection R2688

[*Twelve-wired Bird of Paradise (Seleucidis melanoleuca)*] c.1917
gouache and watercolour on muslin; 16.6 cm diameter
nla.pic–an23712145 Pictures Collection R2687

Cup and saucer with flowering eucalyptus design c.1910–1914
hand painted 'blue ground' porcelain;
cup 5.0 x 9.0 cm; saucer 2.0 cm height, 12.2 cm diameter
Courtesy of the Powerhouse Museum, Sydney

Cup and saucer with flowering eucalyptus design c.1910–1914
hand painted 'blue ground' porcelain;
cup 5.5 x 12.0 cm; saucer 2.0 cm height, 14.5 cm diameter
Courtesy of the Powerhouse Museum, Sydney

'Quaker Edge' plate, two tea plates and a cup and saucer, with various Australian wildflowers   c.1912
hand painted and acid etched porcelain
Courtesy of J.B. Hawkins Photographic Library

[*Bird of Paradise design for the Royal Worcester Porcelain Co. Ltd, London*] c.1916

gouache and watercolour on paper; 23.5 cm diameter

Private collection

Painted screen c.1890
gouache and watercolour on paper and gouache on silk
double-panel hinged screen; each panel 180.5 x 66.5 x 3.5 cm
Gift from the Simpson Family Courtesy of the Board of the Botanic Gardens and State Herbarium, Adelaide

Painted screen c.1890
gouache and watercolour on paper and gouache on silk
double-panel hinged screen; each panel 180.5 x 66.5 x 3.5 cm
Gift from the Simpson Family Courtesy of the Board of the Botanic Gardens and State Herbarium, Adelaide

LIST OF WORKS

Unless otherwise stated all works listed are by Ellis Rowan (1848–1922) and are held in the collections of the National Library of Australia.

Where no formal title for a work exists, the work has been given a descriptive title. These descriptive titles appear in square brackets. Where known, common names for plant specimens have also been included by staff of the National Library of Australia. The locations provided indicate where the painting is believed to have been made.

Ellis Rowan dated only her earliest paintings and also made multiple copies of some images. This makes accurate dating of her work difficult. The circa dates provided are based upon stylistic analysis of both image and surface treatment, plant specimen types (relative to the artist's travels), paper types, inscriptions on reverse by the artist and Ferdinand von Mueller, National Library cataloguers and others.

All measurements are in centimetres, height before width.

Oil Paintings

Chrysanthemums 1888
oil on canvas; 119.5 x 91.5 cm
Winner of First Order of Merit and Gold Medal at the 1888 Centennial International Exhibition, Melbourne Exhibition Building
Private collection, Sydney

Sir John Longstaff (1861–1941)
Memorial Portrait of Mrs Ellis Rowan, Flower Painter and Authoress 1926
oil on canvas; 148.0 x 101.0 cm
nla.pic–an2310713
Pictures Collection R9560

Gouache and Watercolour Paintings

[Drawing of Derriweit Heights, Mount Macedon] c.1873
Mount Macedon, Victoria
gouache and watercolour on paper;
35.0 x 25.0 cm
Courtesy of Mr I. Lindsay, Melbourne

[Christmas Bells (Blandfordia), Flax Lily (Dianella), Haemodorum and Grasses] 1879
Western Australia
gouache and watercolour on paper;
53.7 x 37.2 cm
nla.pic–an6724147
Pictures Collection R2069

[(Abutilon), Emu Bush (Eremophila)] c.1880
Carnarvon, Western Australia
gouache and watercolour on paper;
54.7 x 37.8 cm
nla.pic–an6764648
Pictures Collection R2382

[Black Kangaroo Paw (Macropidia fuliginosa), Red and Green or Mangles' Kangaroo Paw (Anigozanthos manglesii), Cats Paw (Anigozanthos humilis)] c.1880
Perth, Western Australia
gouache and watercolour on paper;
54.7 x 38.0 cm
nla.pic–an6632773
Pictures Collection R2028

[Bluebell (Sollya), Dryandra (Dryandra falcata), Mat Rush (Lomandra endlicheri), Rice Flower (Pimelea)] 1880
Western Australia
gouache and watercolour on paper;
54.5 x 38.0 cm
nla.pic–an6732393
Pictures Collection R2212

[Geebung (Persoonia), Showy Dryandra (Dryandra formosa), (Chorizema diversifolium)] 1880
Albany, Western Australia
gouache and watercolour on paper;
54.4 x 37.9 cm
nla.pic–an6766312
Pictures Collection R2310

[Orchids—Common Spider Orchid (Caladenia patersonii), Blue China Orchid (Caladenia gemmata), Pink Fairies (Caladenia latifolia), Common Donkey Orchid (Diuris longifolia)] 1880
Western Australia
gouache and watercolour on paper;
54.8 x 38.0 cm
nla.pic–an6730524
Pictures Collection R2132

[Rose Cone Flower (Isopogon formosus), Conesticks (Petrophile diversifolia and Petrophile serruriae), Pixie Mops

(Petrophile macrostachya), Cone Bush (Isopogon teretifolia)] 1880
Western Australia
gouache and watercolour on paper;
54.5 x 38.0 cm
nla.pic–an6766367
Pictures Collection R2457

[Trigger Plant (Stylidium), Morning Flag (Orthrosanthus multiflorus), Fan Flower (Scaevola porocarya), Stackhousia, Chamaescilla, Dampiera] 1880
Champion Bay, Western Australia
gouache and watercolour on paper;
54.5 x 38.0 cm
nla.pic–an6765433
Pictures Collection R2384

Ellis Rowan's Garden at Derriweit, Mount Macedon c.1885
Mount Macedon, Victoria
gouache and watercolour on paper;
28.6 x 18.4 cm
nla.pic–an3644559–1
Pictures Collection R9926

Albizzia vaillantii 1887
Johnstone River, Queensland
gouache and watercolour on paper;
54.8 x 38.0 cm
nla.pic–an6730561
Pictures Collection R2142

Bauhinia [Orchid Tree or Mountain Ebony (Bauhinia variegata)] c.1887
Rockhampton, Queensland
gouache and watercolour on paper;
54.8 x 38.1 cm
nla.pic–an6723356
Pictures Collection R2581

[Berries and Fruit] 1887
Johnstone River, Queensland
gouache and watercolour on paper;
54.7 x 38.0 cm
nla.pic–an6766409
Pictures Collection R2625

[Cockatoo or Cocky Apple (Planchonia careya), Morning Glory (Ipomoea sinuata)] c.1887
Dungeness, Herbert River, Queensland
gouache and watercolour on paper;
54.8 x 38.0 cm
nla.pic–an6649745
Pictures Collection R2102

Coleus scuttelarioides, Murdannia graminea, Aneilema gramineum, Commelinaceae c.1887
Queensland
gouache and watercolour on paper;
54.0 x 37.5 cm
nla.pic–an6649803
Pictures Collection R2092

Costus, Artanema fimbriatum, Tabernaemontana pubescens c.1887
Herbert River, Queensland
gouache and watercolour on paper;
54.7 x 38.0 cm
nla.pic–an6732441
Pictures Collection R2239

Crinum longiflora 1887
Queensland
gouache and watercolour on paper;
54.7 x 37.9 cm
nla.pic–an6723088
Pictures Collection R2626

Crinum sp. [Lily] c.1887
Queensland
gouache and watercolour on paper;
56.0 x 38.0 cm
nla.pic–an6649819
Pictures Collection R2096

Cupania erythrocarpa [Tuckeroo], Diploglottis cunninghamii [Native Tamarind] 1887
Johnstone River, Queensland
gouache and watercolour on paper;
54.5 x 38.0 cm
nla.pic–an6723089
Pictures Collection R2624

[Dendrobium discolor] c.1887
Queensland
gouache and watercolour on paper;
54.5 x 38.0 cm
nla.pic–an6732402
Pictures Collection R2218

Dendrobium smillieae [White-flowered variety and Brown Tree Snake 'with a bird just caught between its jaws'] 1887
Mackay, Queensland
gouache and watercolour on paper;
54.7 x 38.0 cm
nla.pic–an6731158
Pictures Collection R2195

Faradaya splendida [Buku] c.1887
Queensland
gouache and watercolour on paper;
54.7 x 38.0 cm
nla.pic–an6723103
Pictures Collection R2618

[Flowers and Fruit] c.1887
Bloomfield, Queensland
gouache and watercolour on paper;
54.7 x 37.8 cm
nla.pic–an6765466
Pictures Collection R2391

Harpullia hillii [Tulipwood], Mackinlaya macrosciadia 1887
Mackay, Queensland
gouache and watercolour on paper;
54.6 x 38.0 cm
nla.pic–an6723385
Pictures Collection R2569

Hibiscus manihot c.1887
Queensland
gouache and watercolour on paper;
54.8 x 38.0 cm
nla.pic–an6649835
Pictures Collection R2106

Melastoma malabathricum [Pink Lasiandra], Wormia alata, Lygodium

scandens [*Maidenhair Fern*] c.1887
Herbert River, Queensland
gouache and watercolour on paper;
54.8 x 38.2 cm
nla.pic–an6731136
Pictures Collection R2180

Mucuna gigantea [*Velvet Bean*], *Nepenthes phyllamphora* [*Pitcher Plant*], *Geitonoplesium cymosum* [*Scrambling Lily*] 1887
Mackay, Queensland
gouache and watercolour on paper;
54.5 x 38.0 cm
nla.pic–an6722787
Pictures Collection R2643

Nelumbo nucifera [*Sacred Lotus or Lotus Lily*] 1887
Herbert River, Queensland
gouache and watercolour on paper;
54.8 x 38.0 cm
nla.pic–an6724357
Pictures Collection R2174

Pandanus pedunculatus [*Beach Pandan*]
1887
Mackay, Queensland
gouache and watercolour on paper;
54.5 x 38.0 cm
nla.pic–an6649839
Pictures Collection R2109

Phaius tankervilliae, Dendrobium cacatua, Dendrobium delicatum c.1887
'Obtained at Brisbane painted in Mackay',
Queensland
gouache and watercolour on paper;
54.7 x 38.0 cm
nla.pic–an6732414
Pictures Collection R2224

[*Rock Lily (Dendrobium speciosum)*] 1887
Queensland
gouache and watercolour on paper;
54.7 x 38.0 cm
nla.pic–an6723370
Pictures Collection R2576

Rubus sp. [*Queensland Bramble (Rubus hillii)*], *Passiflora sp.* [*Passion Flower*], *Tylophora barbata* 1887
Queensland
gouache and watercolour on paper;
54.0 x 38.0 cm
nla.pic–an6735296
Pictures Collection R2269

Tylophora grandiflora, Hemigenia purpurea, Eremophila bignoniflora [*Bignonia Emu Bush*] 1887
Queensland
gouache and watercolour on paper;
54.7 x 38.8 cm
nla.pic–an6723118
Pictures Collection R2608

Xyris pauciflora, Aneilema gramineum, Philydrum lanuginosum [*Woolly Water Lily or Frogsmouth*] 1887
Candollea, Queensland
gouache and watercolour on paper;
54.6 x 37.8 cm
nla.pic–an6731139
Pictures Collection R2183

Flagellaria indica [*Supplejack*], *Barringtonia racemosa* c.1887–1889
Herbert River, Queensland
gouache and watercolour on paper;
54.8 x 38.0 cm
nla.pic–an6722796
Pictures Collection R2635

[*Gymea Lily (Doryanthes excelsa)*]
c.1887–1889
New South Wales (?)
gouache and watercolour on paper;
76.2 x 55.0 cm
nla.pic–an7677462
Pictures Collection R2547

Lygodium sp. and Cardiospermum halicacabum [*Balloon Vine*] c.1887–1889
Queensland (?)
gouache and watercolour on paper;

54.7 x 38.1 cm
nla.pic–an23620907
Pictures Collection R2402

Grevillea leucopteris [*Plume Grevillea*]
c.1889
Western Australia
gouache and watercolour on paper;
53.3 x 35.5 cm
nla.pic–an7719035
Pictures Collection R2436

Halgania corymbosa, Spinifex longifolius, Stylobasium spatulatum c.1889
Carnarvon, Western Australia
gouache and watercolour on paper;
54.0 x 37.3 cm
nla.pic–an6730522
Pictures Collection R2131

Lilac Hibiscus (Alyogyne huegelii) c.1889
Western Australia
gouache and watercolour on paper;
54.7 x 38.0 cm
nla.pic–an6731182
Pictures Collection R2210

Lilac Hibiscus (Alyogyne huegelii) c.1889
Champion Bay, Western Australia
gouache and watercolour on paper;
54.7 x 38.0 cm
nla.pic–an6735435
Pictures Collection R2353

[*Native Hibiscus, Unidentified Flowers and Berries*] c.1889
Western Australia
gouache and watercolour on paper;
54.5 x 38.0 cm
nla.pic–an6766405
Pictures Collection R2616

[*Sturt's Desert Pea (Swainsona formosa)*]
c.1889
Western Australia (?)
gouache and watercolour on paper;
54.5 x 38.0 cm

nla.pic–an23309851
Pictures Collection R2589

[*Royal Botanical Gardens, Melbourne*]
c.1890
Melbourne, Victoria
gouache and watercolour on paper;
27.7 x 65.4 cm
Deakin University Art Collection

Dendrobium atroviolaceum [*Tree Orchid and Forest*] c.1890–1892
Queensland
gouache and watercolour on paper;
55.7 x 38.0 cm
nla.pic–an23620871
Pictures Collection R1805

Evolvulus alsinoides, Lindernia crustacea
c.1890–1892
Queensland
gouache and watercolour on paper;
54.5 x 38.0 cm
nla.pic–an6729725
Pictures Collection R2420

Albizzia lucyi c.1892
Gertrude River, Queensland
gouache and watercolour on paper;
54.8 x 38.2 cm
nla.pic–an6649824
Pictures Collection R2100

Faradaya splendida [*Buku*] c.1892
Queensland
gouache and watercolour on paper;
56.0 x 38.0 cm
nla.pic–an6735287
Pictures Collection R2265

[*Golden Bouquet Tree (Deplanchea tetraphylla)*] c.1892
Somerset, Queensland
gouache and watercolour on paper;
54.5 x 38.0 cm
nla.pic–an6820611
Pictures Collection R2379

[*Gymea Lily (Doryanthes excelsa)*] c.1892
New South Wales (?)
gouache and watercolour on paper;
76.0 x 56.2 cm
nla.pic–an7677432
Pictures Collection R2540

Hibiscus heterophyllus [*Native Rosella*]
c.1892
New South Wales
gouache and watercolour on paper;
55.0 x 38.0 cm
nla.pic–an6724343
Pictures Collection R2179

Ipomoea pandurata [*Wild Jalap*] c.1892
Queensland
gouache and watercolour on paper;
54.7 x 38.0 cm
nla.pic–an6735298
Pictures Collection R2313

[*Old Man or Saw Banksia (Banksia serrata)*] c.1892
Queensland
gouache and watercolour on paper;
76.0 x 56.2 cm
nla.pic–an7677454
Pictures Collection R2543

Passiflora aurantia [*Passionflower*] c.1892
Queensland
gouache and watercolour on paper;
54.5 x 38.0 cm
nla.pic–an6723322
Pictures Collection R2594

[*Screw Pine (Pandanus)*] c.1892
Johnstone River, Queensland
gouache and watercolour on paper;
54.5 x 38.0 cm
nla.pic–an6731160
Pictures Collection R2200

Solanum aculeatissimum c.1892
Inscribed on reverse 'A South American
plant, a naturalised weed in Queensland'

gouache and watercolour on paper;
56.0 x 37.6 cm
nla.pic–an6723081
Pictures Collection R2638

Hoheria populnea [*New Zealand Lacebark*] c.1893
New Zealand
gouache and watercolour on paper;
54.8 x 38.0 cm
nla.pic–an6724275
Pictures Collection R2513

Metrosideros sp. [*New Zealand Christmas Bush*] c.1893
New Zealand
gouache and watercolour on paper;
56.2 x 76.0 cm
nla.pic–an23621177
Pictures Collection R2552

[*Sugar Gum (Eucalyptus cladocalyx)*]
c.1906
South Australia
gouache and watercolour on paper;
73.4 x 54.0 cm
nla.pic–an7677426
Pictures Collection R2536

Bombax malabaricum [*Red Silk Cotton Tree*] c.1911
Queensland
gouache and watercolour on paper;
56.0 x 38.2 cm
nla.pic–an6731148
Pictures Collection R2190

Castanospermum australe [*Black Bean or Moreton Bay Chestnut*] c.1911
Queensland
gouache and watercolour on paper;
56.0 x 38.0 cm
nla.pic–an6732490
Pictures Collection R2242

Eugenia cormiflora c.1911
Barron River, Queensland

gouache and watercolour on paper;
56.0 x 38.0 cm
nla.pic–an6730510
Pictures Collection R2130

Large Tree Orchid with Papilio sp. [*Citrus Butterflies*] c.1911
Queensland
gouache and watercolour on paper;
76.2 x 56.0 cm
nla.pic–an23620971
Pictures Collection R1790

Phaleria macrocarpa c.1911
Queensland
gouache and watercolour on paper;
56.1 x 36.2 cm
nla.pic–an23620968
Pictures Collection R2377

[*Cockatoo or Cocky Apple (Planchonia careya)*] c.1911–1913
Dungeness, Herbert River, Queensland
gouache and watercolour on paper;
55.0 x 38.5 cm
nla.pic–an6729949
Pictures Collection R2474

[*Coral Tree (Erythrina insularis) and Butterflies*] c.1911–1913
Queensland
gouache and watercolour on paper;
55.5 x 38.0 cm
nla.pic–an6647235
Pictures Collection R1849

Coral Tree (Erythrina lysistemon) c.1911–1913
Queensland
gouache and watercolour on paper;
54.7 x 38.0 cm
nla.pic–an6724415
Pictures Collection R2165

Delarbrea michieana c.1911–1913
Queensland
gouache and watercolour on paper;

56.0 x 38.0 cm
nla.pic–an6731151
Pictures Collection R2192

Faradaya splendida [*Buku*]
c.1911–1913
Queensland
gouache and watercolour on paper;
56.0 x 38.0 cm
nla.pic–an6647226
Pictures Collection R1852

Marsh Marigold (Caltha palustris)
c.1911–1913
Queensland
gouache and watercolour on paper;
54.2 x 37.2 cm
nla.pic–an6732410
Pictures Collection R2222

Pimelea haematostachya [*Flinders Poppy*]
c.1911–1913
Queensland
gouache and watercolour on paper;
56.0 x 38.0 cm
nla.pic–an6724418
Pictures Collection R2162

Syzygium sp. c.1911–1913
Queensland
gouache and watercolour on paper;
75.0 x 56.3 cm
nla.pic–an23621312
Pictures Collection R2538

Acalypha sp. with Troides oblongomaculatus [*Birdwing Butterfly*]
c.1916–1917
Papua New Guinea
gouache and watercolour on paper;
76.0 x 55.9 cm
nla.pic–an23621280
Pictures Collection R1757

Amaranthus caudatus [*Tassel Flower*]
c.1916–1917
Papua New Guinea

gouache and watercolour on paper;
78.5 x 60.2 cm
nla.pic–an23621303
Pictures Collection R1922

[*Amorphophallus Flower and Fruit*]
c.1916–1917
Papua New Guinea
gouache and watercolour on paper;
78.3 x 58.7 cm
nla.pic–an6647795
Pictures Collection R1729

Barringtonia sp. with Larva c.1916–1917
Papua New Guinea
gouache and watercolour on paper;
73.3 x 55.8 cm
nla.pic–an23621170
Pictures Collection R1761

Family Araliaceae with Parthenos sylvia [*The Clipper*] c.1916–1917
Papua New Guinea
gouache and watercolour on paper;
76.1 x 55.8 cm
nla.pic–an23621147
Pictures Collection R1759

Freycinetia marginata [*Pandanus*] *with Brown Butterfly* [*Nymphalidae satyridae*]
c.1916–1917
Papua New Guinea
gouache and watercolour on paper;
75.8 x 56.1 cm
nla.pic–an23621188
Pictures Collection R1780

Freycinetia sp. [*Pandanus*] *with Papilio laglaizei* c.1916–1917
Papua New Guinea
gouache and watercolour on paper;
76.2 x 56.0 cm
nla.pic–an23621110
Pictures Collection R1737

Lamiodendron magnificum c.1916–1917
Papua New Guinea

gouache and watercolour on paper;
75.9 x 55.9 cm
nla.pic–an23621201
Pictures Collection R1730

[**Leaves and Flowers of Plant from Papua New Guinea**] c.1916–1917
Papua New Guinea
gouache and watercolour on paper;
76.0 x 56.0 cm
nla.pic–an5597941
Pictures Collection R1791

Maniltoa schefferi c.1916–1917
Papua New Guinea
gouache and watercolour on paper;
76.1 x 56.0 cm
nla.pic–an23621267
Pictures Collection R1787

Pandanus (Freycinetia sp.) c.1916–1917
Papua New Guinea
gouache and watercolour on paper;
75.0 x 54.6 cm
nla.pic–an6647788
Pictures Collection R1747

Pandanus [Freycinetia sp.] c.1916–1917
Papua New Guinea
gouache and watercolour on paper;
76.2 x 55.9 cm
nla.pic–an23621158
Pictures Collection R1795

[**Pendulous Orange Seed Pods**] c.1916–1917
Papua New Guinea
gouache and watercolour on paper;
75.8 x 56.0 cm
nla.pic–an23621128
Pictures Collection R1770

Rubiaceae c.1916–1917
Papua New Guinea
gouache and watercolour on paper;
76.2 x 56.0 cm
nla.pic–an23621261
Pictures Collection R1779

Fungi Paintings

[*Netted Stinkhorn Fungus, Dictyophora phalloidea or Dictyophora multicolor*]
c.1916–1917
(Pair of fungi with dark green and black cap, black lace skirt), Papua New Guinea
gouache and watercolour on paper;
28.0 x 19.0 cm
From the collection of Anna Macgowan

[*Netted Stinkhorn Fungus, Dictyophora phalloidea or Dictyophora multicolor*]
c.1916–1917
(Pair of fungi with grey and black cap, red lace skirt), Papua New Guinea
gouache and watercolour on paper;
28.0 x 19.0 cm
From the collection of Anna Macgowan

[*Netted Stinkhorn Fungus, Dictyophora phalloidea or Dictyophora multicolor*]
c.1916–1917
(Pair of fungi with white and brown cap, gold lace skirt), Papua New Guinea
gouache and watercolour on paper;
28.0 x 19.0 cm
From the collection of Anna Macgowan

[*Netted Stinkhorn Fungus, Dictyophora phalloidea or Dictyophora multicolor*]
c.1916–1917
(Single fungi with black and turquoise cap, turquoise lace skirt), Papua New Guinea
gouache and watercolour on paper;
28.0 x 19.0 cm
From the collection of Anna Macgowan

[*Netted Stinkhorn Fungus, Dictyophora phalloidea or Dictyophora multicolor*]
c.1916–1917
(Single fungi with red and brown cap, mauve lace skirt), Papua New Guinea
gouache and watercolour on paper;
28.0 x 19.0 cm
From the collection of Anna Macgowan

[*Netted Stinkhorn Fungus, Dictyophora phalloidea or Dictyophora multicolor*]
c.1916–1917
(Single fungi with white and olive cap, white lace skirt), Papua New Guinea
gouache and watercolour on paper;
28.0 x 19.0 cm
From the collection of Anna Macgowan

Bird of Paradise Paintings

Brown-headed Paradise Kingfisher (Tanysiptera danae) and Red-breasted Paradise Kingfisher (Tanysiptera nympha)
c.1917
Papua New Guinea
gouache and watercolour on paper;
76.0 x 56.2 cm
nla.pic–an6633351
Pictures Collection R1955

Count Raggi's Bird of Paradise (Paradisaea raggiana) c.1917
Papua New Guinea
gouache and watercolour on paper;
76.0 x 56.0 cm
nla.pic–an6633332
Pictures Collection R1963

[*Elliot's Bird of Paradise*] c.1917
Papua New Guinea
gouache and watercolour on paper;
76.1 x 55.5 cm
nla.pic–an6633334
Pictures Collection R1962

Gorget Bird of Paradise c.1917
Papua New Guinea
gouache and watercolour on paper;
76.0 x 55.8 cm
nla.pic–an6633372
Pictures Collection R1948

Papuan Mynah (Mino dumontii)
c.1917
Papua New Guinea

gouache and watercolour on paper;
75.5 x 56.0 cm
nla.pic–an6633167
Pictures Collection R1976

[*Riflebird*] c.1917
Papua New Guinea
gouache and watercolour on paper;
76.2 x 56.0 cm
nla.pic–an6633165
Pictures Collection R1977

*Rothschild's Bird of Paradise (Astrapia
rothschildi)* c.1917
Papua New Guinea
gouache and watercolour on paper;
76.5 x 56.2 cm
nla.pic–an6633368
Pictures Collection R1949

[*Sickle-tail Bird of Paradise*] c.1917
Papua New Guinea
gouache and watercolour on paper;
76.2 x 55.7 cm
nla.pic–an6633326
Pictures Collection R1966

Bird of Paradise Placemats

[*Brown Sickle-billed Bird of Paradise
(Epimachus meyeri)*] c.1917
gouache and watercolour on muslin;
16.2 cm diameter
nla.pic–an23712209
Pictures Collection R2683

[*Goldie's Bird of Paradise (Paradisaea
decora)*] c.1917
gouache and watercolour on muslin;
16.5 cm diameter
nla.pic–an23715478
Pictures Collection R2688

[*King Birds of Paradise (Cicinnurus
regius)*] c.1917
gouache and watercolour on muslin;

16.7 cm diameter
nla.pic–an23712266
Pictures Collection R2681

[*King of Saxony Bird of Paradise
(Pteridophora alberti)*] c.1917
gouache and watercolour on muslin;
16.5 cm diameter
nla.pic–an6723074–1
Pictures Collection R2686

[*Lawe's Bird of Paradise (Parotia lawesii)*]
c.1917
gouache and watercolour on muslin;
16.4 cm diameter
nla.pic–an23715501
Pictures Collection R2685

[*Lesser Bird of Paradise (Paradisaea
minor)*] c.1917
gouache and watercolour on muslin;
16.8 cm diameter
nla.pic–an23712273
Pictures Collection R2691

[*Magnificent Bird of Paradise (Cicinnurus
magnificus)*] c.1917
gouache and watercolour on muslin;
16.1 cm diameter
nla.pic–an23712280
Pictures Collection R2684

[*Rothschild's Bird of Paradise (Astrapia
rothschildi)*] c.1917
gouache and watercolour on muslin;
16.4 cm diameter
nla.pic–an23715494
Pictures Collection R2689

[*Twelve-wired Bird of Paradise (Seleucidis
melanoleuca)*] c.1917
gouache and watercolour on muslin;
16.6 cm diameter
nla.pic–an23712145
Pictures Collection R2687

Ceramics

The following porcelain ceramics were
produced by the Royal Worcester Porcelain
Company Ltd, London, and were
commissioned and retailed by Flavelle
Brothers, Sydney, from original designs by
Ellis Rowan.

[*Bird of Paradise design for the Royal
Worcester Porcelain Co. Ltd, London*]
c.1916
gouache and watercolour on paper;
23.5 cm diameter
Private collection

**Four plates with flowering eucalyptus
design** c.1910–1914
hand painted 'blue ground' porcelain;
each plate 2.6 cm height, 23.5 cm diameter
Courtesy of the Powerhouse Museum,
Sydney

**Four cups and saucers with flowering
eucalyptus design** c.1911–1912
hand painted 'blue ground' porcelain
cup 5.0 x 9.0 cm (includes handle);
saucer 2.0 cm height, 12.2 cm diameter

cup 5.8 x 12.0 cm (includes handle);
saucer 2.0 cm height, 10.0 cm diameter

cup 4.5 x 9.0 cm (includes handle);
saucer 2.0 cm height, 12.2 cm diameter

cup 5.5 x 12.0 cm (includes handle);
saucer 2.0 cm height, 14.5 cm diameter
Courtesy of the Powerhouse Museum, Sydney

Six 'Quaker Edge' cups and saucers:
*Melaleuca leucadendron, Dianella
elegans, Pultenea, Cremaea violaves,
Exocarpus cupressiformis* (Native
Cherry), *Hibbertia sericea* c.1912
hand painted and acid etched porcelain;
each cup 6.0 cm height, 11.0 cm width
(includes handle); each saucer 2.0 cm height,
12.5 cm diameter
Courtesy of J.B. Hawkins Antiques

Six 'Quaker Edge' plates: *Dendrobium undulata* (Rock Lily), *Cassia brewsteri* (Leichhardt Bean), *Telopea sp.* (Waratah), *Pimelea sp.* (Rice Flower), *Blandfordia cunninghamii* (Christmas Bells), and Flowering Eucalypt c.1912
hand painted and acid etched porcelain;
each plate 2.0 cm height,
23.5 cm diameter
Courtesy of J.B. Hawkins Antiques

Six 'Quaker Edge' tea plates: *Boronia microphylla, Commelina cyanea, Hoheria populnea, Marianthus ringens, Grietina graciliflora, Banksia hookerii* c.1912
hand painted and acid etched porcelain;
each tea plate 2.0 cm height,
15.0 cm diameter
Courtesy of J.B. Hawkins Antiques

Cup and saucer with waratah design
1916–1918
hand painted porcelain; cup 5.0 cm height,
11.0 cm width (includes handle); saucer
2.0 cm height, 12.2 cm diameter
Courtesy of the Powerhouse Museum,
Sydney

Four 'Bird of Paradise' tea plates: *Ranthoniclus aureus, Paradesa aurea, Oriele, Craspedophora magnifica, Paradisea rubra* c.1917
hand painted gilt edged porcelain;
each tea plate 2.5 cm height, 15.5 cm diameter
Courtesy of J.B. Hawkins Antiques

Six 'Bird of Paradise' plates: *Paradisa angustai, Paradisornis rudolphi, Untitled, Lanthotorax bengbachi, Semioptera wallacii* c.1917
hand painted, gilt edged porcelain;
each plate 2.5 cm height, 23.5 cm diameter
Courtesy of J.B. Hawkins Antiques

Six mocha cups and saucers decorated with Australian finches, birds of paradise and a wren c.1917

hand painted porcelain with gilt interior;
each cup 5.5 cm height, 10.0 cm width
(includes handles); each saucer 1.5 cm height,
10.0 cm diameter
Courtesy of J.B. Hawkins Antiques

Painted Screen

Painted screen c.1890
Mount Macedon, Victoria
gouache and watercolour on paper and
gouache on silk
2 double-panel hinged screens;
each panel 180.5 x 66.5 x 3.5 cm
Gift from the Simpson Family
Courtesy of the Board of the Botanic
Gardens and State Herbarium, Adelaide

Medals and Chatelaine

Bronze medal from the International
Exhibition, Victoria 1873
4.6 cm diameter
cast 'Prize Medal' / Incised on rim 'Miss E.
Ryan, Painting'
Private collection

Bronze medal from the International
Exhibition, Sydney 1879
7.5 cm diameter
Private collection

'Special Merit' medal from the
International Exhibition, Sydney 1879
5.0 cm diameter
Incised 'Watercolour painting. Native Flowers.
Special Merit'
Private collection

Medal from the Melbourne International
Exhibition 1880
cast with portrait of Queen Victoria;
7.6 cm diameter
Incised on rim 'Charles Ryan Juror'
Private collection

Silver medal from the International
Colonial Exhibition, Amsterdam 1883
6.9 cm diameter
Private collection

Silver medal from the Calcutta
International Exhibition 1883–1884
5.1 cm diameter
Incised 'Awarded to Mrs Ellis Rowan for
Flower Painting'
Private collection

Bronze medal from the London
International Exhibition, Crystal Palace
1884
6.2 cm diameter
Private collection

Bronze medal from the Colonial and
Indian Exhibition, London 1886
5.2 cm diameter
Incised on reverse 'Head of Albert Edward
Prince of Wales' / Ralph Heaton and Sons,
The Mint Birmingham'
Private collection

Gold medal from the Centennial
International Exhibition, Melbourne 1888
5.1 cm diameter
Incised on rim 'Capt F.C. Rowan'
Private collection

Bronze medal from the World Columbian
Exhibition 1892
(Commemorating the 400th anniversary of
the landing of Christopher Columbus)
7.6 cm diameter
Private collection

Silver chatelaine 1890
three silver chains attached to silver ring
with a belt clip
first chain attached to a silver paint box;
3.0 x 4.0 x 1.2 cm; incised with ornate
initial, 'MER'
second chain attached to a silver brush
holder; 10.5 cm long; incised with ornate

initial 'MER July 1890'
third chain attached to a silver water
bottle; 3.0 x 4.0 x 1.2 cm; incised with
ornate initial, 'MER'
Private collection

Manuscript Items

John Cotton (1801–1849)
Birds Eggs c.1845
watercolour on paper; 17.5 x 12.0 cm
Maie Casey Papers
Manuscript Collection MS1840/9/5

John Cotton (1801–1849)
**The Brown Owl [Southern Boobook
(Ninox novaeseelandiae)]** c.1845
watercolour on paper; 16.5 x 24.5 cm
Maie Casey Papers
Manuscript Collection MS1840/9/5

John Cotton (1801–1849)
**Crested Scrub Bird *Psophodes crepitans*
[Eastern Whipbird (Psophodes olivaceus)]**
c.1845
watercolour on paper; 17.5 x 29.0 cm
Maie Casey Papers
Manuscript Collection MS1840/9/5

Unknown photographer
[Miss Ellis Ryan in a Swiss outfit] 1864
albumen photograph; 22.0 x 16.3 cm
Manuscript Collection MS2206

J. Botterill, Portrait Painter and Photographer
[Ellis Rowan in her wedding dress] 1873
watercolour on paper; 10.5 x 7.9 cm
Pictures Collection R10683

**Dejeuner in celebration of the marriage of
Frederick Charles Rowan and Ellis Ryan,
Vaucluse, Richmond 23 October 1873**
printed and pierced paper; 17.8 x 11.0 cm
Manuscript Collection MS2206

Peince, Photographer
[Ellis Rowan sketching in the garden at

Derriweit Heights **with her son Puck on
his pony and Mary Moule reading]** 1887
albumen photograph; 19.3 x 24.0 cm
nla.pic–an 21411729
Pictures Collection P1064

Private Secretary to Queen Victoria,
Windsor Castle
Letter to Ellis Rowan, 17 May 1895
4 pages of ink on paper;
each page 18.2 x 12.1 cm
Manuscript Collection MS2206

Ferdinand von Mueller (1825–1896)
**Letter to Ellis Rowan, Sunday 1 December
1895**
8 pages of ink on paper;
each page 25.3 x 20.1 cm
Manuscript Collection MS2206

Ellis Rowan's newspaper cuttings book
1895–1922
bound plain paper journal with newsprint
cuttings and other ephemera; 27.8 x 23.0 cm
Manuscript Collection MS2203

George D. Meudell
**Letter regarding 'The Ellis Rowan
collections of water color paintings now on
view in the Art Gallery of Stanford
University, Cal.'** 1919
typescript on paper; 33.0 x 21.5 cm
Manuscript Collection MS2206

Publications

The Picturesque Atlas of Australasia, Volume 3
Sydney: The Picturesque Atlas Publishing
Co., 1886–1888

Ellis Rowan
*A Flower-Hunter in Queensland and New
Zealand*
Sydney: Angus and Robertson, 1898

Alice Lounsberry
(Illustrated by Ellis Rowan)

A Guide to the Wild Flowers
New York: Frederick A. Stokes Company,
1899

Alice Lounsberry
(Illustrated by Ellis Rowan)
Southern Wild Flowers and Trees
New York: Frederick A. Stokes Company,
1901

Ellis Rowan
Bill Baillie: His Life and Adventures
Melbourne: Whitcombe and Tombs, 1908

F. Manson Bailey
*A Comprehensive Catalogue of
Queensland Plants*
Brisbane: A.J. Cumming, Government
Printer, 1913

Henry A. Tardent
*Mrs Ellis Rowan and her Contributions to
Australian Art and Science*
Brisbane: Watson, Ferguson and Co., 1927

Ellis Rowan
Bill Baillie: The Story of a Pet Bilboa
Melbourne: Whitcombe and Tombs Ltd,
1948

Helen Jo Samuel
*Wild Flower Hunter: The Story of Ellis
Rowan*
London: Constable and Company Ltd, 1961

Maie Casey
An Australian Story 1837–1907
London: Michael Joseph Ltd, 1962

Margaret Hazzard and Helen Hewson
*Flower Paintings of Ellis Rowan from the
Collection of the National Library of
Australia*
Canberra: National Library of Australia, 1982

Margaret Hazzard
Australia's Brilliant Daughter, Ellis Rowan:

Artist, Naturalist, Explorer, 1848–1922
Melbourne: Greenhouse Publications,
1984

Geoff Monteith
*The Butterfly Man of Kuranda, Frederick
Parkhurst Dodd*
Brisbane: Queensland Museum, 1991

Ellis Rowan
*The Flower Hunter: The Adventures in
Northern Australia and New Zealand of
the Flower Painter Ellis Rowan*
Sydney: Angus and Robertson, 1991

Christies' London Auction Catalogue
Watercolours and Pictures of Birds and

*Ellis Rowan's Butterflies and Moths of
New Guinea*
London: Christies, Manson and Woods Ltd,
16 May 1995

SELECT BIBLIOGRAPHY

F.M. Bailey, *A Comprehensive Catalogue of Queensland Plants*. Brisbane: A.J. Cumming Government Printer, 1913.

W. Blunt and W.T. Stearn, *The Art of Botanical Illustration*. London: Collins, 1995; London: Antique Collectors' Club, 1994.

M. Casey, *An Australian Story 1837–1907*. London: Michael Joseph, 1962.

M. Casey, *John Cotton 1802–1849*. Pamphlet reprinted for *Journal of the Society for the Bibliography of Natural History*, IV, 2, January 1963.

M. Clarke, *Clarke of Rupertswood (1831–1897)*. Melbourne: Australian Scholarly Publishing, 1995.

K. Collins, *Ellis Rowan 1848–1922: A Biographical Sketch*. Brisbane: Oz Publishing, 1988.

P. de Serville, *Port Phillip Gentlemen*. Melbourne: Oxford University Press, 1980.

J. Gooding, *Margaret Forrest, Wildflowers of Western Australia*. Perth: Art Gallery of Western Australia, 1984.

V. Hammond, *A Century of Australian Women Artists 1840s–1940s*. Melbourne: Deutscher Fine Art, 1993.

M. Hazzard, *Australia's Brilliant Daughter, Ellis Rowan: Artist, Naturalist, Explorer, 1848–1922*. Melbourne: Greenhouse Publications, 1984.

M. Hazzard and H. Hewson, *Flower Paintings of Ellis Rowan from the Collection of the National Library of Australia*. Canberra: National Library of Australia, 1982.

H. Hewson, *Australia: 300 years of Botanical Illustration*. Melbourne: CSIRO Publishing, 1999.

A. Lounsberry, *A Guide to the Wildflowers*. New York: Frederick A. Stokes and Co., 1899.

A. Lounsberry, *A Guide to the Trees*. New York: Frederick A. Stokes and Co., 1900.

A. Lounsberry, *Southern Wild Flowers and Trees*. New York: Frederick A. Stokes and Co., 1901.

G. Mackaness (ed.), *The Correspondence of John Cotton: Victorian Pioneer 1842–1849*. Vol. 30. Dubbo, New South Wales: Australian Historical Monographs, New Series, Review Publications Pty Ltd, 1978. Originally published privately by Dr. George Mackaness in 1956.

J. McKay, *Ellis Rowan: A Flower-Hunter in Queensland*. Brisbane: Queensland Museum, 1990.

J. Nankivell Loch, *A Fringe of Blue: An Autobiography*. London: John Murray, 1968.

M. North, *A Vision of Eden*. London: Webb and Bower, with the Royal Botanical Gardens, Kew, 1980.

E. Rowan, 'Pen and Pencil Notes of a Trip through New Zealand', series in *Australian Town and Country Journal*, 23 December 1893, 11 August 1894.

E. Rowan, *A Flower-Hunter in Queensland and New Zealand*. Sydney: Angus and Robertson, 1898. Reprinted as E. Rowan, *The Flower Hunter: The Adventures in Northern Australia and New Zealand of Flower Painter Ellis Rowan*. Sydney: Angus and Robertson/Harper Collins, 1991.

E. Rowan, 'An Australian Artists' Adventures', series in *New Idea*, 6 January – 5 August 1905.

E. Rowan, *Bill Baillie: His Life and Adventures*. Melbourne: Whitcombe and Tombs, 1908.

E. Rowan, 'Making an Art Collection', in *The Oarswoman*, Brisbane, December 1912.

H.J. Samuel, *Wild Flower Hunter: The Story of Ellis Rowan*. London: Constable and Company, 1961.

H. Sandon, *Royal Worcester Porcelain from 1862 to the Present Day*. London: Barrie and Jenkins, 1973.

H.A. Tardent, *Mrs Ellis Rowan and her Contributions to Australian Art and Science*. Brisbane: Watson, Ferguson and Co., 1927.

R.J. Vane-Wright, 'Watercolours and Pictures of Birds and Ellis Rowan's Butterflies and Moths of New Guinea', in *Christies London Auction Catalogue*. London: Christies, Manson and Woods, 16 May 1995.

H. Vellacott (ed.), *Some Recollections of a Happy Life: Marianne North in Australia and New Zealand*. Melbourne: Edward Arnold Australia, 1986.

ACKNOWLEDGEMENTS

I owe a debt of gratitude to John Wicking and Norman McCann, who first suggested the possibility of this exhibition. It is with deep regret that they are unable to see the results of their enthusiasm as they both died this year. I am also indebted to Patricia Pilfrey who, as research assistant at the National Library of Australia in 1995–1996, documented many sources which laid the groundwork for my initial studies.

Based in Melbourne, I have been fortunate to have supportive friends: Terence Lane (National Gallery of Victoria), Professor Jaynie Anderson (University of Melbourne), Meegan Pannu, Louise Sweetland and David Baillieu, whose library has been a rich resource. I am grateful for the assistance of Jane Macgowan in Sydney and my research in South Australia has been facilitated by Thekla Reichstein and Karen Dankiw (Botanic Gardens of Adelaide and State Herbarium), and Lea Gardam (South Australian Museum).

I am also thankful to Tim Abdullah, Jane Clark, Michael Clarke, Grace Cosgrove (Powerhouse Museum), Mary Eagle, Suzanne Falkiner, John Hawkins, John Jones, Zara Kimpton, Peter Landale, Alan Landis, Mr and Mrs Christopher Lang, Mr and Mrs Andrew Lang, Marjorie Le Souef, Harriet Lester, Ian and Sue Lindsay, Rosemary Lindsay, Joan McClelland, Anna Macgowan, Mary-Jane Malet, Shane McNeice, Raoul Mellish, Ruth Mitchell, Geoff Monteith, Louise Morris, Neil Robertson, Dominic Romeo, Shioban Ryan, Cath Rymill, Paul Tonnoir, Joice Welsh, Dinah Whitaker and Trish Williams.

Finally, I am indebted to Tim Fisher, Nat Williams and the staff at the National Library of Australia, particularly Irene Turpie, Michelle Hetherington, Kathy Jakupec, Greta North, Yvonne Kennedy and to my editor Francesca Rendle-Short who has painlessly adapted my text to fit within these covers.